SECOND EDITION

C# Essentials

Ben Albahari, Peter Drayton,
and Brad Merrill

O'REILLY®

Beijing · Cambridge · Farnham · Köln · Paris · Sebastopol · Taipei · Tokyo

C# Essentials, Second Edition
by Ben Albahari, Peter Drayton, and Brad Merrill

Published by O'Reilly & Associates, Inc., 1005 Gravenstein Highway North,
Sebastopol, CA 95472.

O'Reilly & Associates books may be purchased for educational, business, or sales pro-
motional use. Online editions are also available for most titles (*safari.oreilly.com*). For
more information, contact our corporate/institutional sales department: (800) 998-9938
or *corporate@oreilly.com*.

Editor:	Nancy Wolfe Kotary
Production Editor:	Darren Kelly
Cover Designer:	Ellie Volckhausen
Interior Designer:	David Futato

Printing History:

February 2001:	First Edition.
January 2002:	Second Edition.

ISBN: 0-596-00315-3
[M]

Table of Contents

Preface

C# Essentials is a highly condensed introduction to the C# language and the .NET Framework. C# and the .NET initiative were both unveiled in July 2000 at the Microsoft Professional Developers Conference in Orlando, Florida, and shortly thereafter, the .NET Software Development Kit (SDK) was released on the Internet.

The information in this book is based on Release Candidate 1 (RC1) of the .NET SDK released by Microsoft in October 2001. We expect that version to be largely compatible with the final release, but Microsoft may make minor changes that affect this book. To stay current, be sure to check the online resources listed in the section "C# Online" as well as the O'Reilly web page for this book, *http://www.oreilly.com/catalog/csharpess2* (see the section "How to Contact Us").

Audience

While we have tried to make this book useful to anyone interested in learning about C#, our primary audience is developers already familiar with an object-oriented language such as C++, Smalltalk, Java, or Delphi. C# facilitates writing web applications and services, as well as traditional standalone and client/server-based applications. Experience in any of these areas will make the advantages of C# and the .NET Framework more immediately apparent but isn't required.

About This Book

This book is divided into five chapters and six appendixes:

Chapter 1, *Introduction*, orients you to C# and the .NET Framework.

Chapter 2, *C# Language Reference*, introduces the C# language and serves as a language reference.

Chapter 3, *Programming the .NET Framework*, explains how to use C# and the .NET Framework.

Chapter 4, *Framework Class Library Overview*, provides an overview of the key libraries in .NET—organized by function—and documents the most essential namespaces and types of each.

Chapter 5, *Essential .NET Tools*, is an overview of essential .NET tools that ship with the .NET Framework SDK, including the C# compiler and utilities for importing COM objects and exporting .NET objects.

The six appendixes provide additional information of interest to working programmers, including an alphabetical C# keyword reference, codes for regular expressions and string formats, and a cross reference of assembly and namespace mappings

This book assumes that you have access to the .NET Framework SDK. For additional details on language features and class libraries covered here, we recommend the Microsoft online .NET documentation.

C# Online

Since this book is a condensed introduction to C#, it cannot answer every question you might have about the language. There are many online resources that can help you get the most out of C#.

We recommend the following sites:

http://msdn.microsoft.com/net
> The Microsoft .NET Developer Center is the official site for all things .NET, including the latest version of the .NET Framework SDK, which includes the C# compiler, as well as documentation, technical articles, sample code, pointers to discussion groups, and third-party resources.

http://msdn.microsoft.com/net/thirdparty/default.asp
> A complete list of third-party resources of interest to C# and .NET Framework developers.

http://discuss.develop.com/dotnet.html
> The DevelopMentor DOTNET discussion list. Possibly the best site for freewheeling independent discussion of the .NET languages and framework; participants often include key Microsoft engineers.

http://www.oreillynet.com/dotnet

    The O'Reilly Network .NET DevCenter, which features original articles, news, and weblogs of interest to .NET programmers.

http://dotnet.oreilly.com

    The O'Reilly .NET Center. Visit this page frequently for information on current and upcoming .NET books from O'Reilly. You'll find sample chapters, articles, and other resources.

Two articles of interest include:

http://windows.oreilly.com/news/hejlsberg_0800.html

    An interview with chief C# architect Anders Hejlsberg, by O'Reilly editor John Osborn.

http://www.genamics.com/developer/csharp_comparative.htm

    A comparison of C# to C++ and Java, by coauthor Ben Albahari.

You can find Usenet discussions about .NET in the *microsoft.public.dotnet.** family of newsgroups. In addition, the newsgroup *microsoft.public.dotnet. languages.csharp* specifically addresses C#. If your news server does not carry these groups, you can find them at *news://msnews.microsoft.com*.

Conventions Used in This Book

Throughout this book we use these typographic conventions:

Italic

    Represents the names of system elements, such as directories and files, and Internet resources, such as URLs and web documents. Italics is also used for new terms when they are defined and, occasionally, for emphasis in body text.

`Constant width`

    Indicates language constructs such as .NET and application-defined types, namespaces, and functions, as well as keywords, constants, and expressions that should be typed verbatim. Lines of code and code fragments also appear in constant width, as do classes, class members, and XML tags.

`Constant width italic`

    Represents replaceable parameter names or user-provided elements in syntax.

We have included simple grammar specifications for many, but not all, of the language constructs presented in this book. Our intent is not to be comprehensive—for that level of detail you should consult the Microsoft *C# Programmer's Reference* in the .NET SDK—but rather to provide you with a fast way to understand the grammar of a particular construct and its valid combinations. The XML occurrence operators (?,*, and +) are used to specify more precisely the number of times an element may occur in a particular construct.

x   Indicates x is to be used verbatim (`constant width`)

x   Indicates x is supplied by the programmer (`constant width italic`)

x?   Indicates x may occur zero-or-one times

x*   Indicates x may occur zero-or-more times, separated by commas

x+   Indicates x may occur one-or-more times, separated by commas

[...]

    Indicates a logical grouping of code elements, when not implicitly grouped using the verbatim terms {}, ( ), and [ ]

[x | y]

    Indicates only one of a choice of code elements may occur

This icon designates a note, which is an important aside to the nearby text.

This icon designates a warning relating to the nearby text.

We use the acronym "FCL" to refer to the .NET Framework Class Library. You may have heard this referred to as the Base Class Library in other works, including the first edition of this book.

How to Contact Us

Please address comments and questions concerning this book to the publisher:

O'Reilly & Associates, Inc.
1005 Gravenstein Highway North
Sebastopol, CA 95472
(800) 998-9938 (in the United States or Canada)
(707) 829-0515 (international or local)
(707) 829-0104 (fax)

We have a web page for this book, where we list errata, examples, or any additional information. You can access this page at:

http://www.oreilly.com/catalog/csharpess2

To comment or ask technical questions about this book, send email to:

bookquestions@oreilly.com

For more information about our books, conferences, Resource Centers, and the O'Reilly Network, see our web site at:

http://www.oreilly.com

Acknowledgments

This book would not be possible without the contribution and support of many individuals, including friends, family, and the hard-working folks at O'Reilly & Associates, Inc.

All three of us wish to thank Brian Jepson for his sterling editorial work on the 2nd edition of this book, as well as Jeff Peil for his contributions to the sections of the book that deal with threads and interop. Many thanks as well to Scott Wiltamuth, Joe Nalewabu, Andrew McMullen, and Michael Perry, whose technical reviews have immeasurably improved our text.

Ben Albahari

First of all, I'd like to thank my family (Sonia, Miri, and Joseph Albahari) and friends (most of all Marcel Dinger and Lenny Geros) for still wanting to know me given that I'm practically epoxied to my computer. I'd also like to thank all the bands (can't list them all but particularly Fiona Apple, Dream Theater, and Incubus during this writing period) for the CDs that clutter my desk, without which I would never have been motivated enough to stay up till 5:00 a.m. to simulate being in the same time zone as the great people in America I worked with when writing this book (John Osborn, Peter Drayton, and Brad Merrill). Finally I'd like to thank everyone who is enthusiastic about new technology, which ultimately is what drove me to write this book. I'd like to dedicate this book to my late father, Michael, to whom I am indebted for his foresight in introducing me to programming when I was a child.

Peter Drayton

Above all, I'd like to thank my wife, Julie DuBois, for her constant, loving support. Regardless of how engrossing the world of bits can be, you serve as a constant reminder of how much more wonderful the world of atoms really is. I'd like to thank my coauthors, Ben and Brad, for so graciously affording me the opportunity of participating in this project, and our editor, John Osborn, for keeping all three of us pointed in the same direction during the wild ride that resulted in this book. I'd also like to thank my friends and colleagues (most notably John Prout, Simon Fell, Simon Shortman, and Chris Torkildson) who serve as trusty sounding boards on technical and life issues. Finally, I'd like to thank my family back in South Africa, especially my father, Peter Drayton Sr., and my late mother, Irene Mary Rochford Drayton, for giving me a strong rudder to navigate through life.

Brad Merrill

I'd like to thank my son Haeley, my partner Jodi, my coparent Cyprienne, and my friends (Larry, Colleen, and Evan) for their patience and support during this process. I'd also like to thank Ben and Peter for their immense contributions and our editor John Osborn for keeping us sane.

Introduction

C# is a language built specifically to program the Microsoft .NET Framework. The .NET Framework consists of a runtime environment called the Common Language Runtime (CLR), and a set of class libraries, which provide a rich development platform that can be exploited by a variety of languages and tools.

C# Language

Programming languages have strengths in different areas. Some languages are powerful but can be bug-prone and difficult to work with, while others are simpler but can be limiting in terms of functionality or performance. C# is a new language designed to provide an optimum blend of simplicity, expressiveness, and performance.

Many features of C# were designed in response to the strengths and weaknesses of other languages, particularly Java and C++. The C# language specification was written by Anders Hejlsberg and Scott Wiltamuth. Anders Hejlsberg is famous in the programming world for creating the Turbo Pascal compiler and leading the team that designed Delphi.

Key features of the C# language include the following:

Component orientation
    An excellent way to manage complexity in a program is to subdivide it into several interacting components, some of which can be used in multiple scenarios. C# has been designed to make component building easy and provides component-oriented language constructs such as properties, events, and declarative constructs called *attributes*.

One-stop coding
Everything pertaining to a declaration in C# is localized to the declaration itself, rather than being spread across several source files or several places within a source file. Types do not require additional declarations in separate header or Interface Definition Language (IDL) files, a property's get/set methods are logically grouped, documentation is embedded directly in a declaration, etc. Furthermore, because declaration order is irrelevant, types don't require a separate stub declaration to be used by another type.

Versioning
C# provides features such as explicit interface implementations, hiding inherited members, and read-only modifiers, which help new versions of a component work with older components that depend on it.

Type safety and a unified type system
C# is *type-safe*, which ensures that a variable can be accessed only through the type associated with that variable. This encapsulation encourages good programming design and eliminates potential bugs or security breaches by making it impossible for one variable to inadvertently or maliciously overwrite another.

All C# types (including primitive types) derive from a single base type, providing a *unified type system*. This means all types—structs, interfaces, delegates, enums, and arrays—share the same basic functionality, such as the ability to be converted to a string, serialized, or stored in a collection.

Automatic and manual memory management
C# relies on a runtime that performs automatic memory management. This frees programmers from disposing objects, which eliminates problems such as dangling pointers, memory leaks, and coping with circular references.

However, C# does not eliminate pointers: it merely makes them unnecessary for most programming tasks. For performance-critical hotspots and interoperability, pointers may be used, but they are only permitted in unsafe blocks that require a high security permission to execute.

Leveraging of the CLR
A big advantage of C# over other languages, particularly traditionally compiled languages such as C++, is its close fit with the .NET CLR. Many aspects of C# alias the CLR, especially its type system, memory-management model, and exception-handling mechanism.

Common Language Runtime

Of fundamental importance to the .NET Framework is the fact that programs are executed within a managed execution environment provided by the Common Language Runtime. The CLR greatly improves runtime interactivity between programs, portability, security, development simplicity, and cross-language integration, and provides an excellent foundation for a rich set of class libraries.

Absolutely key to these benefits is the way .NET programs are compiled. Each language targeting .NET compiles source code into *metadata* and Microsoft Intermediate Language (MSIL) code. Metadata includes a complete specification for a program including all its types, apart from the actual implementation of each function. These implementations are stored as MSIL, which is machine-independent code that describes the instructions of a program. The CLR uses this "blueprint" to bring a .NET program to life at runtime, providing services far beyond what is possible with the traditional approach—compiling code directly to assembly language.

Key features of the CLR include the following:

Runtime interactivity
> Programs can richly interact with each other at runtime through their metadata. A program can search for new types at runtime, then instantiate and invoke methods on those types.

Portability
> Programs can be run without recompiling on any operating system and processor combination that supports the CLR. A key element of this platform independence is the runtime's JIT (Just-In-Time) Compiler, which compiles the MSIL code it is fed to native code that runs on the underlying platform.

Security
> Security considerations permeate the design of the .NET Framework. The key to making this possible is CLR's ability to analyze MSIL instructions as being safe or unsafe.

Simplified deployment
> An *assembly* is a completely self-describing package that contains all the metadata and MSIL of a program. Deployment can be as easy as copying the assembly to the client computer.

Versioning
> An assembly can function properly with new versions of assemblies it depends on without recompilation. Key to making this possible is the ability to resolve all type references though metadata.

Simplified development

The CLR provides many features that greatly simplify development, including services such as garbage collection, exception handling, debugging, and profiling.

Cross language integration

The Common Type System (CTS) of the CLR defines the types that can be expressed in metadata and MSIL and the possible operations that can be performed on those types. The CTS is broad enough to support many different languages including Microsoft languages, such as C#, VB.NET, and Visual C++ .NET, and such third-party languages as COBOL, Eiffel, Haskell, Mercury, ML, Oberon, Python, Smalltalk, and Scheme.

The Common Language Specification (CLS) defines a subset of the CTS, which provides a common standard that enables .NET languages to share and extend each other's libraries. For instance, an Eiffel programmer can create a class that derives from a C# class and override its virtual methods.

Interoperability with legacy code

The CLR provides interoperation with the vast base of existing software written in COM and C. .NET types can be exposed as COM types, and COM types can be imported as .NET types. In addition, the CLR provides PInvoke, which is a mechanism that enables C functions, structs, and callbacks to be easily used from within in a .NET program.

Framework Class Library

The .NET Framework provides the .NET Framework Class Library (FCL), which can be used by all languages. The FCL offers features ranging from core functionality of the runtime, such as threading and runtime manipulation of types (reflection), to types that provide high-level functionality, such as data access, rich client support, and web services (whereby code can even be embedded in a web page). C# has almost no built-in libraries; it uses the FCL instead.

A First C# Program

Here is a simple C# program:

```
namespace FirstProgram {
  using System;
  class Test {
```

```
    static void Main () {
      Console.WriteLine ("Welcome to C#!");
    }
  }
}
```

A C# program is composed of types (typically classes) that we organize into namespaces. Each type contains function members (typically methods), as well as data members (typically fields). In our program, we define a class named Test that contains a method, named Main, that writes Welcome to C#! to the Console window. The Console class encapsulates standard input/output functionality, providing methods such as WriteLine. To use types from another namespace, we use the using directive. Since the Console class resides in the System namespace, we write using System; similarly, types from other namespaces could use our Test class by including the following statement: using FirstProgram;.

To compile this program into an executable, paste it into a text file, save it as *Test.cs*, then type **csc Text.cs** in the command prompt. This compiles the program into an executable called *Test.exe*. Add the /debug option to the csc command line to include debugging symbols in the output. This will let you run your program under a debugger and get meaningful stack traces that include line numbers.

 .NET executables contain a small CLR host created by the C# compiler. The host starts the CLR and loads your application, starting at the Main entry point. Note that Main must be specified as static.

In C#, there are no standalone functions; functions are always associated with a type, or as we will see, instances of that type. Our program is simple and makes use of only static members, which means the member is associated with its type, rather than instances of its type. In addition, we make use of only void methods, which means these methods do not return a value. Of final note is that C# recognizes a method named Main as the default entry point of execution.

CHAPTER 2
C# Language Reference

This chapter walks you through each aspect of the C# language. Many features of C# will be familiar if you have experience with a strongly typed object-oriented language.

Identifiers

Identifiers are names programmers choose for their types, methods, variables, and so on. An identifier must be a whole word, essentially composed of Unicode characters starting with a letter or underscore. An identifier must not clash with a keyword. As a special case, the @ prefix can be used to avoid such a conflict, but the character isn't considered part of the identifier that it precedes. For instance, the following two identifiers are equivalent:

```
КоЯn
@КоЯn
```

C# identifiers are case-sensitive, but for compatibility with other languages, you should not differentiate public or protected identifiers by case alone.

Types

A C# program is written by building new *types* and leveraging existing types, either those defined in the C# language itself or imported from other libraries. Each type contains a set of data and function members, which combine to form the modular units that are the key building blocks of a C# program.

Type Instances

Generally, you must create instances of a type to use that type. Those data members and function members that require a type to be *instantiated* are called *instance members*. Data members and function members that can be used on the type itself are called *static members*.

Example: Building and Using Types

In this program, we build our own type called Counter and another type called Test that uses instances of the Counter. The Counter type uses the predefined type int, and the Test type uses the static function member WriteLine of the Console class defined in the System namespace:

```
// Imports types from System namespace, such as Console
using System;
class Counter { // New types are typically classes or structs
  // --- Data members ---
  int value; // field of type int
  int scaleFactor; // field of type int

  // Constructor, used to initialize a type instance
  public Counter(int scaleFactor) {
    this.scaleFactor = scaleFactor;
  }
  // Method
  public void Inc( ) {
    value+=scaleFactor;
  }
  // Property
  public int Count {
    get {return value; }
  }
}
class Test {
  // Execution begins here
  static void Main( ) {

    // Create an instance of counter type
    Counter c = new Counter(5);
    c.Inc( );
    c.Inc( );
    Console.WriteLine(c.Count); // prints "10";

    // Create another instance of counter type
    Counter d = new Counter(7);
    d.Inc( );
    Console.WriteLine(d.Count); // prints "7";
  }
}
```

Implicit and Explicit Conversions

Each type has its own set of rules defining how it can be converted to and from other types. Conversions between types may be implicit or explicit.

Implicit conversions can be performed automatically, while *explicit* conversions require a *cast* using the C cast operator, ( ):

```
int x = 123456; // int is a 4-byte integer
long y = x; // implicit conversion to 8-byte integer
short z =(short)x; // explicit conversion to 2-byte integer
```

The rationale behind implicit conversions is that they are guaranteed to succeed and not lose information. Conversely, an explicit conversion is required when runtime circumstances determine whether the conversion succeeds or when information might be lost during the conversion.

Most conversion rules are supplied by the language, such as the previous numeric conversions. Occasionally it is useful for developers to define their own implicit and explicit conversions (see "Expressions and Operators" later in this chapter).

Categories of Types

All C# types, including both predefined types and user-defined types, fall into one of three categories: *value*, *reference*, and *pointer*.

Value types

Value types typically represent basic types. Simple types, such as basic numeric types (int, long, bool, etc.) are structs, which are value types. You can expand the set of simple types by defining your own structs. In addition, C# allows you to define enums.

Reference types

Reference types typically represent more complex types with rich functionality. The most fundamental C# reference type is the class, but special functionality is provided by the array, delegate, and interface types.

Pointer types

Pointer types fall outside mainstream C# usage and are used only for explicit memory manipulation in unsafe blocks (see "Unsafe Code and Pointers" later in this chapter).

Predefined Types

C# has two categories of predefined types:

- Value types: integers, floating point numbers, decimal, char, bool
- Reference types: object, string

Aliases for all these types can be found in the System namespace. For example, the following two statements are semantically identical:

```
int i = 5;
System.Int32 i = 5;
```

Integral types

The following table describes integral types:

C# type	System type	Size (bytes)	Signed?
sbyte	System.Sbyte	1	Yes
short	System.Int16	2	Yes
int	System.Int32	4	Yes
long	System.Int64	8	Yes
byte	System.Byte	1	No
ushort	System.UInt16	2	No
uint	System.UInt32	4	No
ulong	System.UInt64	8	No

sbyte, short, int, and long are signed integers; byte, ushort, uint, and ulong are unsigned integers.

For unsigned integers n bits wide, their possible values range from 0 to 2^n-1. For signed integers n bits wide, their possible values range from -2^{n-1} to $2^{n-1}-1$. Integer literals can use either decimal or hexadecimal notation:

```
int x = 5;
ulong y = 0x1234AF; // prefix with 0x for hexadecimal
```

When an integral literal is valid for several possible integral types, the chosen default type goes in this order:

```
int
uint
long
ulong.
```

These suffixes may be appended to a value to explicitly specify its type:

U   uint or ulong

L   long or ulong

UL   ulong

Integral conversions. An implicit conversion between integral types is permitted when the resulting type contains every possible value of the type it is converted from. Otherwise, an explicit conversion is required. For instance, you can implicitly convert an int to a long, but must explicitly convert an int to a short:

```
int x = 123456;
long y = x; // implicit, no information lost
short z = (short)x; // explicit, truncates x
```

Floating-point types

C# type	System type	Size (bytes)
float	System.Single	4
double	System.Double	8

A float can hold values from approximately $\pm 1.5 \times 10^{-45}$ to approximately $\pm 3.4 \times 10^{38}$ with seven significant figures.

A double can hold values from approximately $\pm 5.0 \times 10^{-324}$ to approximately $\pm 1.7 \times 10^{308}$ with 15 to 16 significant figures.

Floating-point types can hold the special values +0, –0, +∞, –∞, or NaN (not a number) that represent the outcome of mathematical operations such as division by zero. float and double implement the specification of the IEEE 754 format types, supported by almost all processors, defined at *http://www.ieee.org*.

Floating-point literals can use decimal or exponential notation. A float literal requires the suffix "f" or "F". A double literal may choose to add the suffix "d" or "D".

```
float x = 9.81f;
double y = 7E-02; // 0.07
double z = 1e2;   // 100
```

Floating-point conversions. An implicit conversion from a float to a double loses no information and is permitted but not vice versa. An implicit conversion from an sbyte, short, int, or long (or one of their unsigned counterparts) to a float or double is allowed for readability:

```
short strength = 2;
int offset = 3;
float x = 9.53f * strength - offset;
```

If this example used larger values, precision might be lost. However, the possible range of values isn't truncated because the lowest and highest possible values of a float or double exceed those of any integral type. All other conversions between integral and floating-point types must be explicit:

```
float x = 3.53f;
int offset = (int)x;
```

decimal type

C# type	System type	Size (bytes)
decimal	System.Decimal	16

The decimal type can hold values from $\pm 1.0 \times 10^{-28}$ to approximately $\pm 7.9 \times 10^{28}$ with 28 to 29 significant figures.

The decimal type holds 28 digits and the position of the decimal point on those digits. Unlike a floating-point value, it has more precision but a smaller range. It is typically useful in financial calculations, in which the combination of its high precision and the ability to store a base10 number without rounding errors is valuable. The number 0.1, for instance, is represented exactly with a decimal, but as a recurring binary number with a floating-point type. There is no concept of +0, −0, +∞, −∞, and NaN for a decimal.

A decimal literal requires the suffix "m" or "M":

```
decimal x = 80603.454327m; // holds exact value
```

decimal conversions. An implicit conversion from all integral types to a decimal type is permitted because a decimal type can represent every possible integer value. A conversion from a decimal to floating-point type or vice versa requires an explicit conversion, since floating-point types have a bigger range than a decimal, and a decimal has more precision than a floating-point type.

char type

C# type	System type	Size (bytes)
char	System.Char	2

The char type represents a Unicode character.

A char literal consists of either a character, Unicode format, or escape character enclosed in single quote marks:

```
'A' // simple character
'\u0041' // Unicode
'\x0041' // unsigned short hexadecimal
'\n' // escape sequence character
```

Table 2-1 summarizes the escape characters recognized by C#.

Table 2-1. Escape sequence characters

char	Meaning	Value
\'	Single quote	0x0027
\"	Double quote	0x0022
\\	Backslash	0x005C
\0	Null	0x0000
\a	Alert	0x0007
\b	Backspace	0x0008
\f	Form feed	0x000C
\n	New line	0x000A
\r	Carriage return	0x000D
\t	Horizontal tab	0x0009
\v	Vertical tab	0x000B

char conversions. An implicit conversion from a char to most numeric types works; it's simply dependent on whether the numeric type can accommodate an unsigned short. If it can't, an explicit conversion is required.

bool type

C# type	System type	Size (bytes)
bool	System.Boolean	1/2

The bool type is a logical value, which can be assigned the literal true or false.

Although Boolean values require only 1 bit (0 or 1), they occupy 1 byte of storage since this is the minimum chunk that most processor architectures can allocate. Each element of an array requires 2 bytes of memory.

bool conversions. No conversions can be made from Booleans to numeric types or vice versa.

object type

C# type	System type	Size (bytes)
object	System.Object	0/ 8 overhead

The object type is the ultimate base type for both value types and reference types. Value types have no storage overhead from object. Reference types, which are stored on the heap, intrinsically require an overhead. In the .NET runtime, a reference-type instance has an 8-byte overhead, which stores the object's type and temporary information such as its synchronization lock state or whether it has been fixed from movement by the garbage collector. Note that each reference to a reference-type instance uses 4 bytes of storage.

For more information on the System.Object type, see the section "Common Types" in Chapter 3.

string type

C# type	System type	Size (bytes)
string	System.String	20 minimum

The C# string represents an immutable sequence of Unicode characters and aliases the System.String class (see the section "Strings" in Chapter 3).

Although string is a class, its use is so ubiquitous in programming that it is given special privileges by both the C# compiler and .NET runtime.

Unlike other classes, a new instance can be created with a string literal:

```
string a = "Heat";
```

Strings can also be created with *verbatim* string literals. Verbatim string literals start with a @, which indicates the string should be used verbatim, even if it spans multiple lines or includes escape characters, i.e., "\" (see Table 2-1). In this example the pairs a1 and a2 represent the same string, and the pairs b1 and b2 represent the same string:

```
public void StringDemo( ) {
    string a1 = "\\\\server\\fileshare\\helloworld.cs";
    string a2 = @"\\server\fileshare\helloworld.cs";
    Console.WriteLine(a1==a2); // Prints "True"

    string b1 = "First Line\r\nSecond Line";
    string b2 = @"First Line
Second Line";
    Console.WriteLine(b1==b2); // Prints "True"
}
```

Types and Memory

The fundamental difference between value and reference types is how they are stored in memory.

Memory for value types

The memory of a value-type instance simply holds a raw value, like a number or character. Value types are stored either on the stack or inline. A *stack* is a block of memory that grows each time a method is entered (because its local variables need storage space) and shrinks each time a method exits (because its local variables are no longer needed). *Inline* just means that the value type is declared as part of a larger object, such as when it is a field in a class or a member of an array.

Memory for reference types

The memory of a reference-type instance holds the address of an object on the heap. A reference type may be null, which means no object is referenced. During a program's execution, references are assigned to existing or new objects on the heap. An object on the heap remains in memory until the runtime's garbage collector determines it is no longer referenced, at which time the garbage collector discards the object and releases its memory.

Value types and reference types side by side

To create a value-type or reference-type instance, the constructor for the type may be called with the new keyword. A value-type constructor simply initializes an object. A reference-type constructor creates a new object on the heap and then initializes the object:

```
// Reference-type declaration
class PointR {
  public int x, y;
}
// Value type declaration
struct PointV {
  public int x, y;
}
class Test {
  public static void Main( ) {
    PointR a; // Local reference-type variable, uses 4 bytes of
              // memory on the stack to hold address
    PointV b; // Local value-type variable, uses 8 bytes of
              // memory on the stack for x and y
    a = new PointR( ); // Assigns the reference to address of new
                       // instance of PointR allocated on the
                       // heap. The object on the heap uses 8
                       // bytes of memory for x and y and an
                       // additional 8 bytes for core object
                       // requirements, such as storing the
                       // object's type & synchronization state
    b = new PointV( ); // Calls the value type's default
                       // constructor.  The default constructor
                       // for both PointR and PointV will set
                       // each field to its default value, which
                       // will be 0 for both x and y.
    a.x = 7;
```

only calls the constructor

```
      b.x = 7;
    }
  }
  // At the end of the method the local variables a and b go out of
  // scope, but the new instance of a PointR remains in memory until
  // the garbage collector determines it is no longer referenced
```

Assignment to a reference type copies an object reference; assignment to a value type copies an object value:

```
    ...
    PointR c = a;
    PointV d = b;
    c.x = 9;
    d.x = 9;
    Console.WriteLine(a.x); // Prints 9
    Console.WriteLine(b.x); // Prints 7
  }
}
```

As with this example, an object on the heap can be pointed at by many variables, whereas an object on the stack or inline can be accessed only via the variable it was declared with.

Unified Type System

C# provides a *unified type system*, whereby the object class is the ultimate base type for both reference and value types. This means that all types, apart from the occasionally used pointer types, share a basic set of characteristics.

Simple types are value types

In most languages, there is a strict distinction between simple types (int, float, etc.) and user-defined types (Rectangle, Button, etc.). In C#, simple types actually alias structs found in the System namespace. For instance, the int type aliases the System.Int32 struct, and the long type aliases the System.Int64 struct, etc. This means simple types have the same features you expect any user-defined type to have. For instance, you can call a method on an int:

```
int i = 3;
string s = i.ToString();
```

This is equivalent to:

```
// This is an explanatory version of System.Int32
namespace System {
  struct Int32 {
    ...
    public string ToString() {
      return ...;
```

```
      }
    }
  }
  // This is valid code, but we recommend you use the int alias
  System.Int32 i = 5;
  string s = i.ToString();
```

Value types expand the set of simple types

Creating an array of 1,000 ints is highly efficient. This line allocates 1,000 ints in one contiguous block of memory:

```
int[] iarr = new int [1000];
```

Similarly, creating an array of a value type PointV is also very efficient:

```
struct PointV {
  public int x, y;
}
PointV[] pvarr = new PointV[1000];
```

Had you used a reference type PointR, you would have needed to instantiate 1,000 individual points after instantiating the array:

```
class PointR {
  public int x, y;
}
PointR[] prarr = new PointR[1000];
for( int i=0; i<prarr.Length; i++ )
  prarr[i] = new PointR();
```

In Java, only the simple types (int, float, etc.) can be treated with this efficiency, while in C# you can expand the set of simple types by declaring a struct.

Furthermore, C#'s operators may be overloaded so that operations such as + and −, which are typically applicable to simple types, can also be applied to any class or struct (see "Expressions and Operators" later in this chapter).

Boxing and unboxing value types

In C#, multiple reference types can share the characteristics of a common base type or interface, which allows reference types to be treated generically. This is very powerful. For instance, a method that takes a reference type R for a parameter works for any type that derives from R or implements R (see "Polymorphism" later in this chapter).

To perform common operations on both reference and value types, each value type has a corresponding hidden reference type, which is automatically created when it is cast to a reference type. This process is called *boxing*.

In the following example, the `Queue` class can enqueue and dequeue any object (`object` is a reference type that is the base type of all types). You can put an `int` (a value type) in a queue, because an `int` can be boxed and unboxed to and from its corresponding reference type:

```
class Queue {
  ...
  void Enqueue(object o) {...}
  object Dequeue() {return ...}
}

Queue q = new Queue();
q.Enqueue(9); // box the int
int i = (int)q.Dequeue(); // unbox the int
```

When a value type is boxed, a new reference type is created to hold a copy of the value type. *Unboxing* copies the value from the reference type back into a value type. Unboxing requires an explicit cast, and a check is made to ensure the specified value type matches the type contained in the reference type. An `InvalidCastException` is thrown if the check fails.

> Function members of a value type don't actually override virtual function members of the class `object` or an implemented interface. However, a boxed value type overrides virtual function members.

Variables

A *variable* represents a typed storage location. A variable can be a local variable, a parameter, an array element (see "Arrays" later in this chapter), an instance field, or a static field (see "Instance and Static Members" later in this chapter).

Every variable has an associated type, which essentially defines the possible values the variable can have and the operations that can be performed on that variable. C# is strongly typed, which means the set of operations that can be performed on a type is enforced at compile time, rather than at runtime. In addition, C# is type-safe, which, with the help of runtime checking, ensures that a variable can be operated only via the correct type (except in unsafe blocks; see "Unsafe Code" later in this chapter).

Definite Assignment

Variables in C# (except in unsafe contexts) *must* be assigned a value before they are used. A variable is either explicitly assigned a value or automatically assigned a default value. Automatic assignment occurs for static fields, class instance fields, and array elements not explicitly assigned a value. For example:

```
using System;
class Test {
    int v;
    // Constructors that initialize an instance of a Test
    public Test( ) {} // v will be automatically assigned to 0
    public Test(int a) { // explicitly assign v a value
        v = a;
    }
    static void Main( ) {
        Test[] iarr = new Test [2]; // declare array
        Console.WriteLine(iarr[1]); // ok, elements assigned to null
        Test t;
        Console.WriteLine(t); // error, t not assigned
    }
}
```

Default Values

The following table shows that, essentially, the default value for all primitive (or atomic) types is zero:

Type	Default value
Numeric	0
Bool	false
Char	'\0'
Enum	0
Reference	null

The default value for each field in a complex (or composite) type is one of these aforementioned values.

Expressions and Operators

An expression is a sequence of operators and operands that specifies a computation. C# has unary operators, binary operators, and one ternary operator. Complex expressions can be built because an operand may itself be an expression, such as the operand (1 + 2) in the following example:

```
((1 + 2) / 3)
```

Operator Precedence

When an expression contains multiple operators, the *precedence* of the operators controls the order in which the individual operators are evaluated.

When the operators are of the same precedence, their associativity determines their order of evaluation. Binary operators (except for assignment operators) are *left-associative* and are evaluated from left to right. The assignment operators, unary operators, and the conditional operator are *right-associative*, evaluated from right to left.

For example:

```
1 + 2 + 3 * 4
```

is evaluated as:

```
((1 + 2) + (3 * 4))
```

because * has a higher precedence than +, and + is a left-associative binary operator. You can insert parentheses to change the default order of evaluation. C# also overloads operators, which means the same operator symbols can have different meanings in different contexts (e.g., primary, unary, etc.) or different meanings for different types.

Table 2-2 lists C#'s operators in order of precedence. Operators in the same box have the same precedence, and operators in *italic* may be overloaded for custom types (see "Operators" later in this chapter).

Table 2-2. Operator Precedence Table

Category	Operators
Primary	Grouping: (x) Member access: x.y Struct pointer member access: -> Method call: f(x) Indexing: a[x] *Post increment:* x++ *Post decrement:* x-- Constructor call: new Array stack allocation: stackalloc Type retrieval: typeof Struct size retrieval: sizeof Arithmetic check on: checked Arithmetic check off: unchecked
Unary	*Positive value of (passive):* + *Negative value of:* - *Not:* ! *Bitwise complement:* ~ *Pre increment:* ++x *Pre decrement:* --x Type cast: (T)x Value at address: * Address of value: &

Table 2-2. Operator Precedence Table (continued)

Category	Operators
Multiplicative	*Multiply: ** *Divide: /* *Division remainder: %*
Additive	*Add: +* *Subtract: -*
Shift	*Shift bits left: <<* *Shift bits right: >>*
Relational	*Less than: <* *Greater than: >* *Less than or equal to: <=* *Greater than or equal to: >=* Type equality/compatibility: is Conditional type conversion: as
Equality	*Equals: ==* *Not equals: !=*
Logical bitwise	And: & Exclusive or: ^ Or: |

Logical Boolean	And: &&
	 Or: ||
	 Ternary conditional: ? :
	 e.g. int x = a > b ? 2 : 7;
	 is equivalent to:
	 int x; if (a > b) x = 2; else x = 7;

Assignment	Assign/modify: = *= /= %= += -= <<= >>= &= ^= |=

Arithmetic Overflow Check Operators

Checked/unchecked operator syntax:

```
checked (expression)
unchecked (expression)
```

Checked/unchecked statement syntax:

```
checked statement-or-statement-block
unchecked statement-or-statement-block
```

The checked operator tells the runtime to generate an OverflowException if an integral expression exceeds the arithmetic limits of that type. The checked operator affects expressions with the ++, --, (unary)-, +, -, *, /, and explicit conversion operators () between integral types (see "Integral types" later in this chapter). Here's an example:

```
int a = 1000000;
int b = 1000000;

// Check an expression
int c = checked(a*b);

// Check every expression in a statement block
checked {
    ...
    c = a * b;
    ...
}
```

The checked operator applies only to runtime expressions, because constant expressions are checked during compilation (though this can be turned off with the */checked [+/-]* command-line compiler switch). The unchecked operator disables arithmetic checking at compile time and is seldom useful, but it can enable expressions such as this to compile:

```
const int signedBit = unchecked((int)0x80000000);
```

Statements

Execution of a C# program is specified by a series of *statements* that execute sequentially in the textual order in which they appear. All statements in a procedural-based language such as C# are executed for their effect. The two most basic kinds of statement in C# are the *declaration* and *expression* statements. C# also provides flow control statements for selection, looping, and jumping. Finally, C# provides statements for special purposes, such as locking memory or handling exceptions.

So that multiple statements can be grouped together, zero or more statements may be enclosed in braces ({ }) to form a statement block. A statement block can be used anywhere a single statement is valid.

Expression Statements

Syntax:

[*variable* =]? *expression*;

An *expression statement* evaluates an expression either by assigning its result to a variable or generating side effects, (i.e., invocation, new, ++, or --). An expression statement ends in a semicolon (;). For example:

```
x = 5 + 6; // assign result
x++; // side effect
y = Math.Min(x, 20); // side effect and assign result
Math.Min (x, y); // discards result, but ok, there is a side effect
x == y; // error, has no side effect, and does not assign result
```

Declaration Statements

Variable declaration syntax:

```
type [variable [ = expression ]?]+ ;
```

Constant declaration syntax:

```
const type [variable = constant-expression]+ ;
```

A *declaration statement* declares a new variable. You can initialize a variable at the time of its declaration by optionally assigning it the result of an expression.

The scope of a local or constant variable extends to the end of the current block. You can't declare another local variable with the same name in the current block or in any nested blocks. For example:

```
bool a = true;
while(a) {
    int x = 5;
    if (x==5) {
        int y = 7;
        int x = 2; // error, x already defined
    }
    Console.WriteLine(y); // error, y is out of scope
}
```

A *constant declaration* is like a variable declaration, except that the value of the variable can't be changed after it has been declared:

```
const double speedOfLight = 2.99792458E08;
speedOfLight+=10; // error
```

Empty Statements

Syntax:

```
;
```

The *empty statement* does nothing. It is used as a placeholder when no operations need to be performed, but a statement is nevertheless required. For example:

```
while(!thread.IsAlive);
```

Selection Statements

C# has many ways to conditionally control the flow of program execution. This section covers the simplest two constructs, the if-else statement and the switch statement. In addition, C# also provides a conditional operator and loop statements that conditionally execute based on a Boolean expres-

sion. Finally, C# provides object-oriented ways of conditionally controlling
the flow of execution, namely virtual method invocations and delegate invocations.

if-else statement

Syntax:

```
if (Boolean-expression)
  statement-or-statement-block
[ else
  statement-or-statement-block ]?
```

An if-else statement executes code depending on whether a Boolean
expression is true. Unlike C, C# permits only a Boolean expression. For
example:

```
int Compare(int a, int b) {
    if (a>b)
        return 1;
    else if (a<b)
        return -1;
    return 0;
}
```

switch statement

Syntax:

```
switch (expression) {
[ case constant-expression : statement* ]*
[ default : statement* ]?
}
```

switch statements let you branch program execution based on the value of a
variable. switch statements can result in cleaner code than if you use multiple if statements, because the controlling expression is evaluated only once.
For instance:

```
void Award(int x) {
  switch(x) {
    case 1:
      Console.WriteLine("Winner!");
      break;
    case 2:
      Console.WriteLine("Runner-up");
      break;
    case 3:
    case 4:
      Console.WriteLine("Highly commended");
      break;
    default:
```

```
      Console.WriteLine("Don't quit your day job!");
      break;
  }
}
```

The switch statement can evaluate only a predefined type (including the string type) or enum, though user-defined types may provide an implicit conversion to these types.

After a particular case statement is executed, control doesn't automatically continue to the next statement or break out of the switch statement. Instead, you must explicitly control execution, typically by ending each case statement with a jump statement. The options are:

- Use the break statement to jump to the end of the switch statement (this is by far the most common option).
- Use the goto case <*constant expression*> or goto default statements to jump to either another case statement or the default case statement.
- Use any other jump statement, namely return, throw, continue, or goto *label*.

Unlike in Java and C++, the end of a case statement must explicitly state where to go next. There is no error-prone "default fall through" behavior, so not specifying a jump statement results in the next case statement being executed:

```
void Greet(string title) {
  switch (title) {
    case null:
      Console.WriteLine("And you are?");
      goto default;
    case "King":
      Console.WriteLine("Greetings your highness");
      // error, should specify break, otherwise...
    default :
      Console.WriteLine("How's it hanging?");
      break;
  }
}
```

Loop Statements

C# enables a group of statements to be executed repeatedly using the while, do while, and for statements.

while loops

Syntax:

```
while (Boolean-expression)
  statement-or-statement-block
```

while loops repeatedly execute a statement block while a given Boolean expression remains true. The expression is tested before the statement block is executed:

```
int i = 0;
while (i<5) {
  i++;
}
```

do-while loops

Syntax:

```
do
  statement-or-statement-block
while (Boolean-expression);
```

do-while loops differ functionally from while loops only in that they test the controlling Boolean expression after the statement block has executed. Here's an example:

```
int i = 0;
do
  i++;
while (i<5);
```

for loops

Syntax:

```
for (statement?; Boolean-expression?; statement?)
  statement-or-statement-block
```

for loops can be more convenient than while loops when you need to maintain an iterator value. As in Java and C, for loops contain three parts. The first part is a statement executed before the loop begins, and by convention, it initializes an iterator variable. The second part is a Boolean expression that, while true, permits the statement block to execute. The third part is a statement that is executed after each iteration of the statement block and, by convention, increments an iterator variable. Here's an example:

```
for (int i=0; i<10; i++)
  Console.WriteLine(i);
```

Any of the three parts of the for statement may be omitted. You can implement an infinite loop like this, though alternatively a while (true) statement has the same result:

```
for (;;)
  Console.WriteLine("Hell ain't so bad");
```

foreach loops

Syntax:

```
foreach ( type-value in IEnumerable )
  statement-or-statement-block
```

It's common to use for loops to iterate over a collection, so C#, like Visual Basic, includes a foreach statement. For instance, instead of doing this:

```
for (int i=0; i<dynamite.Length; i++)
  Console.WriteLine(dynamite [i]);
```

you can do this:

```
foreach (Stick stick in dynamite)
  Console.WriteLine(stick);
```

The foreach statement works on any collection (including arrays). Although not strictly necessary, all collections leverage this functionality by implementing the IEnumerable and IEnumerator interfaces, which are explained in the section "Collections" in Chapter 3. Here is an equivalent way to iterate over the collection:

```
IEnumerator ie = dynamite.GetEnumerator();
while (ie.MoveNext()) {
  Stick stick = (Stick)ie.Current;
  Console.WriteLine(stick);
}
```

jump Statements

The C# jump statements are: break, continue, goto, return, and throw. All jump statements obey sensible restrictions imposed by try statements (see the section "try Statements and Exceptions" later in this chapter). First, a jump out of a try block always executes the try's finally block before reaching the target of the jump. Second, a jump can't be made from the inside to the outside of a finally block.

break statement

Syntax:

```
break;
```

The break statement transfers execution from the enclosing while loop, for loop, or switch statement block to the next statement block:

```
int x = 0;
while (true) {
  x++;
  if (x>5)
    break; // break from the loop
}
```

continue statement

Syntax:

```
continue;
```

The continue statement forgoes the remaining statements in the loop and makes an early start on the next iteration:

```
int x = 0;
int y = 0;
while (y<100) {
  x++;
  if ((x%7)==0)
    continue; // continue with next iteration
  y++;
}
```

goto statement

Syntax:

```
goto statement-label;
goto case-constant;
```

The goto statement transfers execution to another *label* within the statement block. A label statement is just a placeholder in a method:

```
int x = 4;
start:
x++;
if (x==5)
  goto start;
```

The goto case statement transfers execution to another case *label* in a switch block (as explained in the "switch statement" section).

return statement

Syntax:

```
return expression?;
```

The return statement exits a method. If the method is non-void, it must return an expression of the method's return type:

```
int CalcX(int a) {
  int x = a * 100;
  return x; // return to the calling method with value
}
```

throw statement

Syntax:

```
throw exception-expression?;
```

The throw statement throws an Exception to indicate that an abnormal condition has occurred (see "try Statements and Exceptions" later in this chapter):

```
if (w==null)
  throw new Exception("w can't be null");
```

lock statement

Syntax:

```
lock (expression)
  statement-or-statement-block
```

The lock statement is actually a syntactic shortcut for calling the Enter and Exit methods of the Monitor class (see "Threading" in Chapter 3).

using statement

Syntax:

```
using (declaration-expression)
  statement-or-statement-block
```

Many classes encapsulate non-memory resources, such as file handles, graphics handles, or database connections. These classes implement System.IDisposable, which defines a single parameterless method named Dispose that is called to clean up these resources. The using statement provides an elegant syntax for declaring, then calling, the Dispose method of variables that implement IDisposable. For example:

```
using (FileStream fs = new FileStream (fileName, FileMode.Open)) {
  // do something with fs
}
```

This is precisely equivalent to:

```
FileStream fs = new FileStream (fileName, FileMode.Open);
try {
```

```
    // do something with fs
} finally {
  if (fs != null)
  ((IDisposable)fs).Dispose( );
}
```

Organizing Types

A C# program is basically a group of types. These types are defined in *files*, organized by *namespaces*, compiled into *modules*, and then grouped into an *assembly*.

Generally, these organizational units overlap: an assembly can contain many namespaces, and a namespace can be spread across several assemblies. A module can be part of many assemblies, and an assembly can contain many modules. A source file can contain many namespaces, and a namespace can span many source files. For more information, see the section "Assemblies" in Chapter 3.

Files

File organization is of almost no significance to the C# compiler: an entire project can be merged into a single *.cs* file and still compile successfully (preprocessor statements are the only exception to this). However, it's generally tidy to have one type in one file, with a filename that matches the name of the class and a directory name that matches the name of the class's namespace.

Namespaces

Namespace declaration syntax:

```
namespace name+ª {
  using-statement*
  [namespace-declaration | type-declaration]*ᵇ
}
```

ª Dot-delimited.
ᵇ No delimiters.

A namespace enables you to group related types into a hierarchical categorization. Generally the first name in a namespace name is the name of your organization, followed by names that group types with finer granularity. For example:

```
namespace MyCompany.MyProduct.Drawing {
  class Point {int x, y, z;}
  delegate void PointInvoker(Point p);
}
```

Nesting namespaces

You may also nest namespace declarations instead of using dots. This example is semantically identical to the previous example:

```
namespace MyCompany {
  namespace MyProduct {
    namespace Drawing {
      class Point {int x, y, z;}
      delegate void PointInvoker(Point p);
    }
  }
}
```

Using a type with its fully qualified name

The complete name of a type includes its namespace name. To use the Point class from another namespace, you may refer to it with its fully qualified name:

```
namespace TestProject {
  class Test {
    static void Main( ) {
      MyCompany.MyProduct.Drawing.Point x;
    }
  }
}
```

using keyword

The using keyword is a convenient way to avoid using the fully qualified names of types in other namespaces. This example is semantically identical to the previous example:

```
namespace TestProject {
  using MyCompany.MyProduct.Drawing;
  class Test {
    static void Main( ) {
      Point x;
    }
  }
}
```

Aliasing types and namespaces

Type names must be unique within a namespace. To avoid naming conflicts without having to use fully qualified names, C# allows you to specify an alias for a type or namespace. Here is an example:

```
using sys = System;       // Namespace alias
using txt = System.String; // Type alias
class Test {
```

```
static void Main( ) {
  txt s = "Hello, World!";
  sys.Console.WriteLine(s); // Hello, World!
  sys.Console.WriteLine(s.GetType( )); // System.String
  }
}
```

Global namespace

The outermost level within which all namespaces and types are implicitly declared is called the *global namespace*. When a type isn't explicitly declared within a namespace, it can be used without qualification from any other namespace, since it is a member of the global namespace. However, it is always good practice to organize types within logical namespaces

Inheritance

A C# class can *inherit* from another class to extend or customize that class. A class can inherit only from a single class but can be inherited by many classes, thus forming a class hierarchy. At the root of any class hierarchy is the object class, which all objects implicitly inherit from. Inheriting from a class requires specifying the class to inherit from in the class declaration, using the C++ colon notation:

```
class Location { // Implicitly inherits from object
  string name;

  // The constructor that initializes Location
  public Location(string name) {
    this.name = name;
  }
  public string Name {get {return name;}}
  public void Display( ) {
    Console.WriteLine(Name);
  }
}
class URL : Location { // Inherit from Location
  public void Navigate( ) {
    Console.WriteLine("Navigating to "+Name);
  }
  // The constructor for URL, which calls Location's constructor
  public URL(string name) : base(name) {}
}
```

URL has all the members of Location and a new member, Navigate:

```
class Test {
  public static void Main( ) {
    URL u = new URL("http://microsoft.com");
    u.Display( );
```

```
      u.Navigate( );
   }
}
```

 The specialized class and general class are referred to as either the *derived class* and *base class* or the *subclass* and *superclass*.

Class Conversions

A class D may be implicitly *upcast* to the class B it derives from, and a class B may be explicitly *downcast* to a class D that derives from it. For instance:

```
URL u = new URL("http://microsoft.com");
Location l = u; // upcast
u = (URL)l; // downcast
```

If the downcast fails, an `InvalidCastException` is thrown.

as operator

The as operator allows a downcast that evaluates to `null` to be made if the downcast fails:

```
u = l as URL;
```

is operator

The is operator can test if an object is or derives from a specified class (or implements an interface). It is often used to perform a test before a downcast:

```
if (l is URL)
  ((URL)l).Navigate( );
```

Polymorphism

Polymorphism is the ability to perform the same operation on many types, as long as each type shares a common subset of characteristics. C# custom types exhibit polymorphism by inheriting classes and implementing interfaces (see "Interfaces" later in this chapter).

In the following example, the Show method can perform the operation Display on both a URL and a LocalFile because both types inherit the characteristics of Location:

```
class LocalFile : Location {
  public void Execute( ) {
    Console.WriteLine("Executing "+Name);
  }
```

```
    // The constructor for LocalFile, which calls Location's constructor
    public LocalFile(string name) : base(name) {}
}
class Test {
  static void Main( ) {
    URL u = new URL("http://www.microsoft.com");
    LocalFile l = new LocalFile("C:\\LOCAL\\README.TXT");
    Show(u);
    Show(l);
  }
  public static void Show(Location loc) {
    Console.Write("Location is: ");
    loc.Display( );
  }
}
```

Virtual Function Members

A key aspect of polymorphism is that each type can implement a shared characteristic in its own way. One way to permit such flexibility is for a base class to declare function members as virtual. Derived classes can provide their own implementations for any function members marked virtual in the base class (see "Interfaces" later in this chapter):

```
class Location {
  public virtual void Display( ) {
    Console.WriteLine(Name);
  }
  ...
}
class URL : Location {
  // chop off the http:// at the start
  public override void Display( ) {
    Console.WriteLine(Name.Substring(7));
  }
  ...
}
```

URL now has a custom way of displaying itself. The Show method of the Test class in the previous section will now call the new implementation of Display. The signatures of the overridden method and the virtual method must be identical, but unlike Java and C++, the override keyword is also required.

Abstract Classes and Members

A class can be declared *abstract*. An abstract class may have abstract members, which are function members without implementation that are implicitly virtual. In earlier examples, we specified a Navigate method for the URL type and an `Execute` method for the `LocalFile` type. You can, instead, declare `Location` an abstract class with an abstract method called `Launch`:

```
abstract class Location {
  public abstract void Launch();
}
class URL : Location {
  public override void Launch() {
    Console.WriteLine("Run Internet Explorer...");
  }
}
class LocalFile : Location {
  public override void Launch() {
    Console.WriteLine("Run Win32 Program...");
  }
}
```

A derived class must override all its inherited abstract members or must itself be declared abstract. An abstract class can't be instantiated. For instance, if `LocalFile` doesn't override `Launch`, `LocalFile` itself must be declared abstract, perhaps to allow `Shortcut` and `PhysicalFile` to derive from it.

Sealed Methods and Sealed Classes

An overridden function member may seal its implementation so it cannot be overridden. In our previous example, we could have made the `URL`'s implementation of `Display` sealed. This prevents a class that derives from `URL` from overriding `Display`, which provides a guarantee on the behavior of a `URL`.

```
public sealed override void Display() {...}
```

A class can prevent other classes from inheriting from it by specifying the sealed modifier in the class declaration:

```
sealed class Math {
  ...
}
```

The most common scenario for sealing a class is when that class comprises only static members, as is the case with the `Math` class of the FCL. Another effect of sealing a class is that it enables the compiler to seal all virtual method invocations made on that class into faster, nonvirtual method invocations.

Hiding Inherited Members

Aside from its use for calling a constructor, the new keyword can also hide the data members, function members, and type members of a base class.

Overriding a virtual method with the new keyword hides, rather than overrides, the base class implementation of the method:

```
class B {
  public virtual void Foo() {
    Console.WriteLine("In B.");
  }
}
class D : B {
  public override void Foo() {
    Console.WriteLine("In D.");
  }
}
class N : D {
  public new void Foo() {  // hides D's Foo
    Console.WriteLine("In N.");
  }
}
public static void Main() {
  N n = new N();
  n.Foo();  // calls N's Foo
  ((D)n).Foo();  // calls D's Foo
  ((B)n).Foo();  // calls D's Foo
}
```

A method declaration with the same signature as its base class should explicitly state whether it overrides or hides the inherited member.

Versioning Virtual Function Members

In C#, a method is compiled with a flag that is true if the method overrides a virtual method. This flag is important for versioning. Suppose you write a class that derives from a base class in the .NET Framework and then deploy your application to a client computer. The client later upgrades the .NET Framework, and the .NET base class now contains a virtual method that happens to match the signature of one of your methods in the derived class:

```
public class Base {  // written by the library people
  public virtual void Foo() {...}  // added in latest update
}
public class Derived : Base {  // written by you
  public void Foo() {...}  // not intended as an override
}
```

In most object-oriented languages, such as Java, methods are not compiled with this flag, so a derived class's method with the same signature is *assumed* to override the base class's virtual method. This means a virtual call is made to type Derived's Foo method, even though Derived's Foo is unlikely to have been implemented according to the specification intended by the author of type Base. This can easily break your application. In C#, the flag for Derived's Foo will be false, so the runtime knows to treat Derived's Foo as new, which ensures that your application will function as it was originally intended. When you get the chance to recompile with the latest framework, you can add the new modifier to Foo, or perhaps rename Foo something else.

Access Modifiers

To promote encapsulation, a type or type member may hide itself from other types or other assemblies by adding one of the following five access modifiers to the declaration:

public
> The type or type member is fully accessible. This is the implicit accessibility for enum members (see "Enums" later in this chapter) and interface members (see "Interfaces" later in this chapter).

internal
> The type or type member in assembly A is accessible only from within A. This is the default accessibility for nonnested types, so it may be omitted.

private
> The type member in type T is accessible only from within T. This is the default accessibility for class and struct members, so it may be omitted.

protected
> The type member in class C is accessible only from within C or from within a class that derives from C.

protected internal
> The type member in class C and assembly A is accessible only from within C, from within a class that derives from C, or from within A. Note that C# has no concept of protected and internal, in which a type member in class C and assembly A is accessible only from within C or from within a class that derives from C and is within A.

Note that a type member may be a nested type. Here is an example that uses access modifiers:

```
// Assembly1.dll
using System;
public class A {
  private int x=5;
  public void Foo( ) {Console.WriteLine (x);}
  protected static void Goo( ) {}
  protected internal class NestedType {}
}
```

```
internal class B {
  private void Hoo () {
    A a1 = new A (); // ok
    Console.WriteLine(a1.x); // error, A.x is private
    A.NestedType n; // ok, A.NestedType is internal
    A.Goo(); // error, A's Goo is protected
  }
}

// Assembly2.exe (references Assembly1.dll)
using System;
class C : A { // C defaults to internal
  static void Main() { // Main defaults to private
    A a1 = new A(); // ok
    a1.Foo(); // ok
    C.Goo(); // ok, inherits A's protected static member
    new A.NestedType(); // ok, A.NestedType is protected
    new B(); // error, Assembly 1's B is internal
    Console.WriteLine(x); // error, A's x is private
  }
}
```

Restrictions on Access Modifiers

A type or type member can't declare itself to be more accessible than any of the types it uses in its declaration. For instance, a class can't be public if it derives from an internal class, or a method can't be protected if the type of one of its parameters is internal to the assembly. The rationale behind this restriction is that whatever is accessible to another type is actually usable by that type.

In addition, access modifiers can't be used when they conflict with the purpose of inheritance modifiers. For example, a virtual (or abstract) member can't be declared private, since it would then be impossible to override. Similarly, a sealed class can't define new protected members, since there is no class that can benefit from this accessibility.

Finally, to maintain the contract of a base class, a function member with the override modifier must have the same accessibility as the virtual member it overrides.

Classes and Structs

Class declaration syntax:

attributes? unsafe? *access-modifier*?
new?
[abstract | sealed]?

Class declaration syntax:

```
class class-name
[: base-class | : interface+ | : base-class, interface+ ]?
{ class-members }
```

Struct declaration syntax:

```
attributes? unsafe? access-modifier?
new?
struct struct-name [: interface+]?
{ struct-members }
```

A class or struct combines data, functions, and nested types into a new type, which is a key building block of C# applications. The body of a class or struct is comprised of three kinds of members: data, function, and type.

Data members

> Includes fields, constants, and events. The most common data members are fields. Events are a special case, since they combine data and functionality in the class or struct (see "Events" later in this chapter).

Function members

> Includes methods, properties, indexers, operators, constructors, and destructors. Note that all function members are either specialized types of methods or are implemented with one or more specialized types of methods.

Type members

> Includes nested types. Types can be nested to control their accessibility (see "Access Modifiers" later in this chapter).

Here's an example:

```
class ExampleClass {
    int x; // data member
    void Foo( ) {} // function member
    struct MyNestedType  {} // type member
}
```

Differences Between Classes and Structs

Classes differ from structs in the following ways:

- A class is a reference type; a struct is a value type. Consequently, structs are typically simple types in which value semantics are desirable (e.g., assignment copies a value rather than a reference).
- A class fully supports inheritance (see "Inheritance" earlier in this chapter). A struct inherits from object and is implicitly sealed. Both classes and structs can implement interfaces.

Structs are implicitly Sealed, [handwritten annotation]

- A class can have a destructor; a struct can't.
- A class can define a custom parameterless constructor and initialize instance fields; a struct can't. The default parameterless constructor for a struct initializes each field with a default value (effectively zero). If a struct declares a constructor(s), all its fields must be assigned in that constructor call.

Instance and Static Members

Data members and function members may be either instance (default) or static members. Instance members are associated with an instance of a type, whereas static members are associated with the type itself. Furthermore, invocation of static members from outside their enclosing type requires specifying the type name. In this example, the instance method `PrintName` prints the name of a particular `Panda`, while the static method `PrintSpeciesName` prints the name shared by all `Pandas` in the application (`AppDomain`):

```
using System;
class Panda {
  string name;
  static string speciesName = "Ailuropoda melanoleuca";
  // Initializes Panda (see the later section "Instance Constructors")
  public Panda(string name) {
    this.name = name;
  }
  public void PrintName() {
    Console.WriteLine(name);
  }
  public static void PrintSpeciesName() {
    Console.WriteLine(speciesName);
  }
}
class Test {
  static void Main() {
    Panda.PrintSpeciesName(); // invoke static method
    Panda p = new Panda("Petey");
    p.PrintName(); // invoke instance method
  }
}
```

Fields

Syntax:

attributes? unsafe? *access-modifier*?
new?
static?

Syntax:

```
[readonly | volatile]?
type [ field-name [ = expression]? ]+ ;
```

Fields hold data for a class or struct. Fields are also referred to as member variables:

```
class MyClass {
  int x;
  float y = 1, z = 2;
  static readonly int MaxSize = 10;
  ...
}
```

As the name suggests, the readonly modifier ensures a field can't be modified after it's assigned. Such a field is termed a *read-only field*. Assignment to a read-only field is always evaluated at runtime, not at compile time. To compile, a read-only field's assignment must occur in its declaration or within the type's constructor (see "Instance Constructors" later in this chapter). Both read-only and non–read-only fields generate a warning when left unassigned.

The volatile modifier indicates that a field's value may be modified in a multi-threaded scenario, and that neither the compiler nor the runtime should perform optimizations with that field.

Constants

Syntax:

```
attributes? access-modifier?
new?
const type [ constant-name = constant-expression ]+;
```

The *type* must be one of the following predefined types: sbyte, byte, short, ushort, int, uint, long, ulong, float, double, decimal, bool, char, string, or enum.

A *constant* is a field that is evaluated at compile time and is implicitly static. The logical consequence of this is that a constant can't defer evaluation to a method or constructor and can only be one of a few built-in types (see the preceding syntax definition).

```
public const double PI = 3.14159265358979323846;
```

The benefit of a constant is that since it is evaluated at compile time, the compiler can perform additional optimization. For instance:

```
public static double Circumference(double radius) {
  return 2 * Math.PI * radius;
}
```

evaluates to:

```
public static double Circumference(double radius) {
   return 6.28318530717959 * radius;
}
```

Versioning with constants

A readonly field isn't optimized by the compiler but is more versionable. For instance, suppose there is a mistake with PI, and Microsoft releases a patch to their library that contains the Math class, which is deployed to each client computer. If software using the Circumference method is already deployed on a client machine, the mistake isn't fixed until you recompile your application with the latest version of the Math class. With a readonly field, however, this mistake is automatically fixed the next time the client application is executed. Generally this scenario occurs when a field value changes not as a result of a mistake, but simply because of an upgrade, such as a change in the value of the MaxThreads constant from 500 to 1,000.

Properties

Syntax:

```
attributes? unsafe? access-modifier?
[
   [[sealed | abstract]? override] |
   new? [virtual | abstract | static]?
]?
type property-name { [
   attributes? get statement-block |    // read-only
   attributes? set statement-block |    // write-only
   attributes? get statement-block      // read-write
   attributes? set statement-block
] }
```

abstract accessors don't specify an implementation, so they replace a get/set block with a semicolon. Also see "Restrictions on Access Modifiers" earlier in this chapter.

A *property* can be characterized as an object-oriented field. Properties promote encapsulation by allowing a class or struct to control access to its data and by hiding the internal representation of the data. For instance:

```
public class Well {
   decimal dollars; // private field
   public int Cents {
      get { return(int)(dollars * 100); }
      set {
         // value is an implicit variable in a set
         if (value>=0) // typical validation code
```

```
            dollars = (decimal)value/100;
        }
      }
    }
    class Test {
      static void Main( ) {
          Well w = new Well( );
          w.Cents = 25; // set
          int x = w.Cents; // get
          w.Cents += 10; // get and set(throw a dime in the well)
      }
    }
```

The get accessor returns a value of the property's type. The set accessor has an implicit parameter value that is of the property's type.

> Many languages loosely implement properties with a get or set method convention, and in fact, C# properties are compiled to get_XXX or set_XXX methods, which is their representation in MSIL; for example:
>
> ```
> public int get_Cents {...}
> public void set_Cents (int value) {...}
> ```
>
> Simple property accessors are inlined by the JIT (just-in-time compiler), which means there is no performance difference between a property access and a field access. Inlining is an optimization that replaces a method call with the body of that method.

Indexers

Syntax:

```
attributes? unsafe? access-modifier?
[
  [[sealed | abstract]? override] |
  new? [virtual | abstract]?
]?
type this [ attributes? [type arg]+ ] {
  attributes? get statement-block |   // read-only
  attributes? set statement-block |   // write-only
  attributes? get statement-block     // read-write
  attributes? set statement-block
}
```

abstract accessors don't specify an implementation, so they replace a get/set block with a semicolon. Also see "Restrictions on Access Modifiers" earlier in this chapter.

An *indexer* provides a natural way to index elements in a class or struct that encapsulates a collection, using the open and closed bracket ([ ]) syntax of the array type. For example:

```
public class ScoreList {
  int[] scores = new int [5];
  // indexer
  public int this[int index] {
    get {
      return scores[index]; }
    set {
      if(value >= 0 && value <= 10)
        scores[index] = value;
    }
  }
  // property (read-only)
  public int Average {
    get {
      int sum = 0;
      foreach(int score in scores)
        sum += score;
      return sum / scores.Length;
    }
  }
}
class IndexerTest {
  static void Main() {
    ScoreList sl = new ScoreList();
    sl[0] = 9;
    sl[1] = 8;
    sl[2] = 7;
    sl[3] = sl[4] = sl[1];
    System.Console.WriteLine(sl.Average);
  }
}
```

A type may declare multiple indexers that take different parameters.

Indexers are compiled to get_Item (...)/set_Item (...) methods, which is their representation in MSIL:

```
public Story get_Item (int index) {...}
public void set_Item (int index, Story value) {...}
```

Consequently, you cannot define a property named Item in a type that has an indexer.

Methods

Method declaration syntax:

attributes? unsafe? *access-modifier*?
[

Method declaration syntax:

```
[[sealed | abstract]? override] |
new? [ virtual | abstract | static extern? ]?
]?
[ void | type ] method-name (parameter-list)
statement-block
```

Parameter list syntax:

```
[ attributes? [ref | out]? type arg ]*
[ params attributes? type[] arg ]?
```

abstract and extern methods don't contain a method body. Also see "Restrictions on Access Modifiers" earlier in this chapter.

All C# code executes in a *method* or in a special form of a method (constructors, destructors, and operators are special types of methods, and properties and indexers are internally implemented with get/set methods).

Signatures

A method's *signature* is characterized by the type and modifier of each parameter in its parameter list. The parameter modifiers ref and out allow arguments to be passed by reference rather than by value.

Passing arguments by value

By default, arguments in C# are passed by value, which is by far the most common case. This means a copy of the value is created when passed to the method:

```
static void Foo(int p) {++p;}
public static void Main( ) {
  int x = 8;
  Foo(x); // make a copy of the value type x
  Console.WriteLine(x); // x will still be 8
}
```

Assigning p a new value doesn't change the contents of x, since p and x reside in different memory locations.

ref modifier

To pass by reference, C# provides the parameter modifier ref. Using this modifier allows p and x to refer to the same memory locations:

```
static void Foo(ref int p) {++p;}
public static void Test( ) {
  int x = 8;
  Foo(ref x); // send reference of x to Foo
  Console.WriteLine(x); // x is now 9
}
```

Now, assigning p a new value changes the contents of x. This is usually why you want to pass by reference, though occasionally it is an efficient technique with which to pass large structs. Notice how the `ref` modifier is required in the method call, as well as in the method declaration. This makes it very clear what's going on and removes ambiguity since parameter modifiers change the signature of a method (see "Signatures" earlier in this chapter).

out modifier

C# is a language that enforces the requirement that variables be assigned before use, so it also provides the out modifier, which is the natural complement of the ref modifier. While a `ref` modifier requires that a variable be assigned a value before being passed to a method, the out modifier requires that a variable be assigned a value before returning from a method:

```
using System;
class Test {
  static void Split(string name, out string firstNames,
                    out string lastName) {
    int i = name.LastIndexOf(' ');
    firstNames = name.Substring(0, i);
    lastName = name.Substring(i+1);
  }
  public static void Main( ) {
    string a, b;
    Split("Nuno Bettencourt", out a, out b);
    Console.WriteLine("FirstName:{0}, LastName:{1}", a, b);
  }
}
```

params modifier

The params parameter modifier may be specified on the last parameter of a method so the method can accept any number of parameters of a particular type. For example:

```
using System;
class Test {
  static int Add(params int[] iarr) {
    int sum = 0;
    foreach(int i in iarr)
      sum += i;
    return sum;
  }
  static void Main( ) {
    int i = Add(1, 2, 3, 4);
    Console.WriteLine(i); // 10
  }
}
```

Overloading methods

A type may overload methods (have multiple methods with the same name) as long as the signatures are different.[*] For example, the following methods can coexist in the same type:

```
void Foo(int x);
viod Foo(double x);
void Foo(int x, float y);
void Foo(float x, int y);
void Foo(ref int x);
```

However, the following pairs of methods can't coexist in the same type, since the return type and params modifier don't qualify as part of a method's signature:

```
void Foo(int x);
float Foo(int x); // compile error
void Goo (int[] x);
void Goo (params int[] x); // compile error
```

Operators

Overloadable operators:

```
+ - ! ~ ++ -- + -
* (binary only) / % & (binary only)
| ^ << >> ++ != > <
>= <= ==
```

Literals doubling as overloadable operators:

```
true false
```

C# lets you overload operators to work with operands that are custom classes or structs using operators. An *operator* is a static method with the keyword operator preceding the operator to be overloaded (instead of a method name), parameters representing the operands, and return type representing the result of an expression.

Implementing value equality

A pair of references exhibit referential equality when both references point to the same object. By default, the == and != operators will compare two reference-type variables by reference. However, it is ocassionally more natural

---

[*] A minor exception to this rule is that two otherwise identical signatures cannot coexist if one parameter has the ref modifier and the other parameter has the out modifier.

for the == and != operators to exhibit value equality, whereby the comparison is based on the value of the objects that the references point to.

Whenever overloading the == and != operators, you should always override the virtual Equals method to route its functionality to the == operator. This allows a class to be used polymorphically (which is essential if you want to take advantage of functionality such as the collection classes). It also provides compatibility with other .NET languages that don't overload operators.

 A good guideline for knowing whether to implement the == and != operators is if it is natural for the class to overload other operators too, such as <, >, +, or -; otherwise, don't bother—just implement the Equals method. For structs, overloading the == and != operators provides a more efficient implementation than the default one.

```
using System;
class Note {
  int value;
  public Note(int semitonesFromA) {
    value = semitonesFromA;
  }
  public static bool operator ==(Note x, Note y) {
    return x.value == y.value;
  }
  public static bool operator !=(Note x, Note y) {
    return x.value != y.value;
  }
  public override bool Equals(object o) {
    if(!(o is Note))
      return false;
    return this ==(Note)o;
  }
  public static void Main( ) {
    Note a = new Note(4);
    Note b = new Note(4);
    Object c = a;
    Object d = b;

    // To compare a and b by reference:
    Console.WriteLine((object)a ==(object)b); // false

    // To compare a and b by value:
    Console.WriteLine(a == b); // true

    // To compare c and d by reference:
    Console.WriteLine(c == d); // false

    // To compare c and d by value:
```

```
      Console.WriteLine(c.Equals(d)); // true
   }
}
```

Logically paired operators

The C# compiler enforces the rule that operators that are logical pairs must both be defined. These operators are == and !=; < and >; and <= and >=.

Custom implicit and explicit conversions

As explained in the earlier section "Types," the rationale behind *implicit* conversions is they are guaranteed to succeed and not lose information during the conversion. Conversely, an *explicit* conversion is required either when runtime circumstances determine if the conversion succeeds or if information is lost during the conversion. In the following example, we define conversions between the musical Note type and a double (which represents the frequency in hertz of that note):

```
...
// Convert to hertz
public static implicit operator double(Note x) {
   return 440*Math.Pow(2,(double)x.value/12);
}

// Convert from hertz (accurate only to nearest semitone)
public static explicit operator Note(double x) {
   return new Note((int)(0.5+12*(Math.Log(x/440)/Math.Log(2))));
}
...

Note n =(Note)554.37; // explicit conversion
double x = n; // implicit conversion
```

Three-state logic operators

The true and false keywords are used as operators when defining types with *three-state logic* to enable these types to seamlessly work with constructs that take Boolean expressions, namely the if, do, while, for, and conditional (?:) statements. The System.Data.SQLTypes. SQLBoolean struct provides this functionality:

```
public struct SQLBoolean ... {
   int value;
   ...
   public SQLBoolean(int value) {
      this.value = value;
   }
   public static bool operator true(SQLBoolean x) {
      return x.value == 1;
   }
```

```
    public static bool operator false(SQLBoolean x) {
      return x.value == -1;
    }
    public static SQLBoolean operator !(SQLBoolean x) {
      return new SQLBoolean(- x.value);
    }
    public bool IsNull {
      get { return value == 0;}
    }
    ...
  }
  class Test {
    public static void Foo(SQLBoolean a) {
      if (a)
        Console.WriteLine("True");
      else if (! a)
        Console.WriteLine("False");
      else
        Console.WriteLine("Null");
    }
  }
```

Indirectly overloadable operators

The && and || operators are automatically evaluated from & and |, so they don't need to be overloaded. The [] operators can be customized with indexers (see "Indexers" earlier in this chapter). The assignment operator = can't be overloaded, but all other assignment operators are automatically evaluated from their corresponding binary operators (e.g., += is evaluated from +).

Instance Constructors

Syntax:

attributes? unsafe? *access-modifier*?
unsafe?
class-name (*parameter-list*)
[:[base | this] (*argument-list*)]?
statement-block

An *instance constructor* allows you to specify the code to be executed when a class or struct is instantiated. A class constructor first creates a new instance of that class on the heap and then performs initialization, while a struct constructor merely performs initialization.

Unlike ordinary methods, a constructor has the same name as the class or struct in which it is declared, and has no return type:

```
class MyClass {
  public MyClass( ) {
```

```
      // initialization code
   }
}
```

A class or struct can overload constructors and may call one of its over-loaded constructors before executing its method body using the this key-word:

```
using System;
class MyClass {
   public int x;
   public MyClass() : this(5) {}
   public MyClass(int v) {
      x = v;
   }
   public static void Main() {
      MyClass m1 = new MyClass();
      MyClass m2 = new MyClass(10);
      Console.WriteLine(m1.x); // 5
      Console.WriteLine(m2.x); // 10;
   }
}
```

If a class does not define any constructors, an implicit parameterless con-structor is created. A struct can't define a parameterless constructor, since a constructor that initializes each field with a default value (effectively zero) is always implicitly defined.

Calling base class constructors

A class constructor must call one of its base class constructors first. In the case where the base class has a parameterless constructor, that constructor is called implicitly. In the case where the base class provides only constructors that require parameters, the derived class constructor must explicitly call one of the base class constructors using the base keyword. A constructor may also call an overloaded constructor (which calls base for it):

```
class B {
   public int x ;
   public B(int a) {
      x = a;
   }
   public B(int a, int b) {
      x = a * b;
   }
   // Notice that all of B's constructors need parameters
}
class D : B {
   public D() : this(7) {} // call an overloaded constructor
   public D(int a) : base(a) {} // call a base class constructor
}
```

Field initialization order

Another useful way to perform initialization is to assign fields an initial value in their declaration:

```
class MyClass {
  int x = 5;
}
```

Field assignments are performed before the constructor is executed and are initialized in the textual order in which they appear. For classes, every field assignment in each class in the inheritance chain is executed before any of the constructors are executed, from the least derived to the most derived class.

Constructor access modifiers

A class or struct may choose any access modifier for a constructor. It is occasionally useful to specify a private constructor to prevent a class from being constructed. This is appropriate for utility classes made up entirely of static members, such as the System.Math class.

Static Constructors

Syntax:

attributes? unsafe? extern?
static *class-name* ( )
statement-block

Note that extern static constructors don't specify an implementation, so they replace a statement-block with a semicolon.

A *static constructor* allows initialization code to be executed before the first instance of a class or struct is created, or before any static member of the class or struct is accessed. A class or struct can define only one static constructor, and it must be parameterless and have the same name as the class or struct:

```
class Test {
  static Test() {
    Console.WriteLine("Test Initialized");
  }
}
```

Base class constructor order

Consistent with instance constructors, static constructors respect the inheritance chain, so each static constructor from the least derived to the most derived is called.

Static field initialization order

Consistent with instance fields, each static field assignment is made before any of the static constructors is called, and the fields are initialized in the textual order in which they appear:

```
class Test {
  public static int x = 5;
  public static void Foo( ) {}
  static Test( ) {
    Console.WriteLine("Test Initialized");
  }
}
```

Accessing either Test.x or Test.Foo assigns 5 to x and prints Test Initialized.

Nondeterminism of static constructor calls

Static constructors can't be called explicitly, and the runtime may invoke them well before they are first used. Programs shouldn't make any assumptions about the timing of a static constructor's invocation. In the following example, Test Initialized can be printed after Test2 Initialized:

```
class Test2 {
  public static void Foo( ) {}
  static Test2( ) {
    Console.WriteLine("Test2 Initialized");
  }
}
...
Test.Foo( );
Test2.Foo( );
```

Self-Referencing

C# provides the keywords for accessing the members of a class itself or of the class from which it is derived, namely the this and base keywords.

this keyword

The this keyword denotes a variable that is a reference to a class or struct instance and is accessible only from within nonstatic function members of the class or struct. The this keyword is also used by a constructor to call an overloaded constructor (see "Instance Constructors" earlier in this chapter) or declare or access indexers (see "Indexers" earlier in this chapter). A common use of the this variable is to unambiguate a field name from a parameter name:

```
class Dude {
  string name;
```

```
public Dude(string name) {
  this.name = name;
}
public void Introduce(Dude a) {
  if (a!=this)
    Console.WriteLine("Hello, I'm "+name);
}
}
```

base keyword

The base keyword is similar to the this keyword, except that it accesses an overridden or hidden base-class function member. The base keyword can also call a base-class constructor (see "Instance Constructors" earlier in this chapter) or access a base-class indexer (using base instead of this). Calling base accesses the next most derived class that defines that member. To build upon the example with the this keyword:

```
class Hermit : Dude {
  public Hermit(string name): base(name) {}
  public new void Introduce(Dude a) {
    base.Introduce(a);
    Console.WriteLine("Nice Talking To You");
  }
}
```

 There is no way to access a specific base-class instance member, as with the C++ scope resolution :: operator.

Destructors and Finalizers

Syntax:

attributes? unsafe?
~*class-name* ( )
statement-block

Destructors are class-only methods used to clean up non-memory resources just before the garbage collector reclaims the memory for an object. Just as a constructor is called when an object is created, a destructor is called when an object is destroyed. C# destructors are very different from C++ destructors, primarily because of the garbage collector's presence. First, memory is automatically reclaimed with a garbage collector, so a destructor in C# is solely used for non-memory resources. Second, destructor calls are non-deterministic. The garbage collector calls an object's destructor when it determines it is no longer referenced. However, it may determine that this is an undefined period of time after the last reference to the object disappeared.

The C# compiler expands a destructor into a `Finalize` method override:

```
protected override void Finalize() {
  ...
  base.Finalize();
}
```

For more details on the garbage collector and finalizers, see "Automatic Memory Management" in Chapter 3.

Nested Types

A *nested type* is declared within the scope of another type. Nesting a type has three benefits:

- It can access all the members of its enclosing type, regardless of a member's access modifier.
- It can be hidden from other types with type-member access modifiers.
- Accessing a nested type from outside its enclosing type requires specifying the type name (same principle as static members).

Here's an example of a nested type:

```
using System;
class A {
  int x = 3; // private member
  protected internal class Nested {// choose any access level
    public void Foo () {
      A a = new A ();
      Console.WriteLine (a.x); // can access A's private members
    }
  }
}
class B {
  static void Main () {
    A.Nested n = new A.Nested (); // Nested is scoped to A
    n.Foo ();
  }
}
// an example of using "new" on a type declaration
class C : A {
  new public class Nested {} // hide inherited type member
}
```

 Nested classes in C# are roughly equivalent to static inner classes in Java. There is no C# equivalent to Java's nonstatic inner classes, in which an inner class has a reference to an instance of the enclosing class.

Interfaces

Syntax:

```
attributes? unsafe? access-modifier?
new?
interface interface-name [ : base-interface+ ]?
{ interface-members }
```

An interface is like a class, but with these major differences:

- An interface provides a specification rather than an implementation for its members. This is similar to a pure `abstract` class, which is an abstract class consisting of only abstract members.

- A class and struct can implement multiple interfaces; a class can inherit only from a single class.

- A struct can implement an interface but can't inherit from a class.

Earlier we defined polymorphism as the ability to perform the same operations on many types, as long as each type shares a common subset of characteristics. The purpose of an interface is precisely for defining such a set of characteristics.

An interface is comprised of one or more methods, properties, indexers, and events. These members are always implicitly public and implicitly abstract (therefore virtual and nonstatic).

Defining an Interface

An interface declaration is like a class declaration, but it provides no implementation for its members, since all its members are implicitly abstract. These members are intended to be implemented by a class or struct that implements the interface.

Here's a simple interface that defines a single method:

```
public interface IDelete {
  void Delete();
}
```

Implementing an Interface

Classes or structs that implement an interface may be said to "fulfill the contract of the interface." In this example, GUI controls that support the concept of deleting, such as a `TextBox` or `TreeView`, or your own custom GUI control, can implement the `IDelete` interface:

```
public class TextBox : IDelete {
  public void Delete() {...}
```

```
    }
    public class TreeView : IDelete {
      public void Delete( ) {...}
    }
```

If a class inherits from a base class, the name of each interface to be implemented must appear after the base-class name:

```
    public class TextBox : Control, IDelete {...}
    public class TreeView : Control, IDelete {...}
```

Using an Interface

An interface is useful when you need multiple classes to share characteristics not present in a common base class. In addition, an interface is a good
way to ensure that these classes provide their own implementation for the
interface member, since interface members are implicitly abstract.

The following example assumes a form containing many GUI controls,
including some TextBox and TreeView controls, in which the currently
focused control is accessed with the ActiveControl property. When a user
clicks Delete on a menu item or a toolbar button, you test to see if
ActiveControl implements IDelete, and if so, cast it to IDelete to call its
Delete method:

```
    class MyForm {
      ...
      void DeleteClick( ) {
        if (ActiveControl is IDelete) {
          IDelete d = (IDelete)ActiveControl;
          d.Delete( );
        }
      }
    }
```

Extending an Interface

Interfaces may extend other interfaces. For instance:

```
    interface ISuperDelete : IDelete {
      bool CanDelete {get;}
      event EventHandler CanDeleteChanged;
    }
```

In implementing the ISuperDelete interface, an ActiveControl implements
the CanDelete property to indicate it has something to delete and isn't read-
only. The control also implements the CanDeleteChanged event to fire an
event whenever its CanDelete property changes. This framework lets the

application ghost its Delete menu item and toolbar button when the ActiveControl is unable to delete.

Explicit Interface Implementation

If there is a name collision between an interface member and an existing member in the class or struct, C# allows you to explicitly implement an interface member to resolve the conflict. In this example, we resolve a conflict that arises when we implement two interfaces that each define a Delete method:

```
public interface IDesignTimeControl {
   ...
   object Delete( );
}
public class TextBox : IDelete, IDesignTimeControl {
   ...
   void IDelete.Delete( ) {...}
   object IDesignTimeControl.Delete( ) {...}
   // Note that explicitly implementing just one of them would
   // be enough to resolve the conflict
}
```

Unlike implicit interface implementations, explicit interface implementations can't be declared with abstract, virtual, override, or new modifiers. In addition, they are implicitly public, while an implicit implementation requires the use of the public modifier. However, to access the method, the class or struct must be cast to the appropriate interface first:

```
TextBox tb = new TextBox( );
IDesignTimeControl idtc = (IDesignTimeControl)tb;
IDelete id = (IDelete)tb;
idtc.Delete( );
id.Delete( );
```

Reimplementing an Interface

If a base class implements an interface member with the virtual (or abstract) modifier, a derived class can override it. If not, the derived class must reimplement the interface to override that member:

```
public class RichTextBox : TextBox, IDelete {
   // TextBox's IDelete.Delete is not virtual (since explicit
   // interface implementations cannot be virtual)
   public void Delete( ) {}
}
```

The implementation in this example lets you use a RichTextBox object as an IDelete object and call RichTextBox's version of Delete.

Interface Conversions

A class or struct T can be implicitly cast to an interface I that T implements. Similarly, an interface X can be implicitly cast to an interface Y that X inherits from. An interface can be explicitly cast to any other interface or nonsealed class. However, an explicit cast from an interface I to a sealed class or struct T is permitted only if T can implement I. For example:

```
interface IDelete {...}
interface IDesignTimeControl {...}
class TextBox : IDelete, IDesignTimeControl {...}
sealed class Timer : IDesignTimeControl {...}

TextBox tb1 = new TextBox ();
IDelete d = tb1; // implicit cast
IDesignTimeControl dtc = (IDesignTimeControl)d;
TextBox tb2 = (TextBox)dtc;
Timer t = (Timer)d; // illegal, a Timer can never implement IDelete
```

Standard boxing conversions happen when converting between structs and interfaces.

Arrays

Syntax:

type[*]+ *array-name* = new type [*dimension+*][*]*;

Note that [*] is the set: [] [,] [,,] ...

Arrays allow a group of elements of a particular type to be stored in a contiguous block of memory. Array types derive from System.Array and are declared in C# using brackets ([ ]). For instance:

```
char[] vowels = new char[] {'a','e','i','o','u'};
Console.WriteLine(vowels [1]); // Prints "e"
```

The preceding function call prints "e" because array indexes start at 0. To support other languages, .NET can create arrays based on arbitrary start indexes, but the FCL libraries always use zero-based indexing. Once an array has been created, its length can't be changed. However, the System.Collection classes provide dynamically sized arrays, as well as other data structures, such as associative (key/value) arrays (see "Collections" in Chapter 3).

Multidimensional Arrays

Multidimensional arrays come in two varieties, rectangular and jagged. *Rectangular* arrays represent an *n*-dimensional block; *jagged* arrays are arrays of arrays:

```
// rectangular
int [,,] matrixR = new int [3, 4, 5]; // creates one big cube
// jagged
int [][][] matrixJ = new int [3][][];
for (int i = 0; i < 3; i++) {
    matrixJ[i] = new int [4][];
    for (int j = 0; j < 4; j++)
        matrixJ[i][j] = new int [5];
}
// assign an element
matrixR [1,1,1] = matrixJ [1][1][1] = 7;
```

Local and Field Array Declarations

For convenience, *local* and *field declarations* can omit the array type when assigning a known value, because the type is specified in the declaration:

```
int[,] array = {{1,2},{3,4}};
```

Array Length and Rank

Arrays know their own length. For multidimensional arrays, the `GetLength` method returns the number of elements for a given dimension, which is counted from 0 (the outermost) to the array's Rank-1 (the innermost):

```
// one-dimensional
for(int i = 0; i < vowels.Length; i++);
// multidimensional
for(int i = 0; i < matrixR.GetLength(2); i++);
```

Bounds Checking

All array indexing is bounds-checked by the CLR, with `IndexOutOf-RangeException` thrown for invalid indexes. As in Java, *bounds checking* prevents program faults and debugging difficulties while enabling code to be executed with security restrictions.

> Generally the performance hit from bounds checking is minor, and the JIT can perform optimizations such as determining each array index is safe before entering a loop, thus avoiding a check made for each iteration. In addition, C# provides unsafe code to explicitly bypass bounds checking (see "Unsafe Code and Pointers" later in this chapter).

Array Conversions

Arrays of reference types can be converted to other arrays using the same logic you apply to its element type (this is called *array covariance*). All arrays implement System.Array, which provides methods to generic get and set elements regardless of array type.

Enums

Syntax:

```
attributes? access-modifier?
new?
enum enum-name [ : integer type ]?
{ [attributes? enum-member-name [ = value ]? ]* }
```

Enums specify a group of named numeric constants:

```
public enum Direction {North, East, West, South}
```

Unlike in C, enum members must be used with the enum type name. This resolves naming conflicts and makes code clearer:

```
Direction walls = Direction.East;
```

By default, enums are assigned integer constants: 0, 1, 2, etc. You can optionally specify an alternative numeric type to base your enum on and explicitly specify values for each enum member:

```
[Flags]
public enum Direction : byte {
    North=1, East=2, West=4, South=8
}
Direction walls = Direction.North | Direction.West;
if((walls & Direction.North) != 0)
    System.Console.WriteLine("Can't go north!");
```

The [Flags] attribute is optional. It informs the runtime that the values in the enum can be bit-combined and should be decoded accordingly in the debugger or when outputting text to the console. For example:

```
Console.WriteLine(walls); // Displays "North, West"
Console.WriteLine(walls.ToString("d")); // displays "5"
```

The System.Enum type also provides many useful static methods for enums that allow you to determine the underlying type of an enum, check if a specific value is supported, initialize an enum from a string constant, retrieve a list of the valid values, and perform other common operations such as conversions. Here is an example:

```
using System;
public enum Toggle : byte { Off=0, On=1 }
```

```
class TestEnum {
  static void Main( ) {
    Type t = Enum.GetUnderlyingType(typeof(Toggle));
    Console.WriteLine(t); // Prints "System.Byte"

    bool bDimmed = Enum.IsDefined(typeof(Toggle), "Dimmed");
    Console.WriteLine(bDimmed); // Prints "False"

    Toggle tog =(Toggle)Enum.Parse(typeof(Toggle), "On");
    Console.WriteLine(tog.ToString("d")); // Prints "1"
    Console.WriteLine(tog); // Prints "On"

    Array oa = Enum.GetValues(typeof(Toggle));
    foreach(Toggle atog in oa) // Prints "Off=0, On=1"
      Console.WriteLine("{0}={1}", atog, atog.ToString("d"));
  }
}
```

Enum Operators

The operators relevant to enums are:

==	!=	< >	<=	&
>=	+	-	^	|
-=	+=	=	++	~
sizeof	--			

Enum Conversions

Enums can be explicitly converted to other enums. Enums and numeric types can be explicitly converted to one another. A special case is the numeric literal 0, which can be implicitly converted to an enum.

Delegates

Syntax:

attributes? unsafe? *access-modifier*?
new?
delegate
[void | *type*]
delegate-name (*parameter-list*);

A *delegate* is a type that defines a method signature so delegate instances can hold and invoke a method or list of methods that match its signature. A delegate declaration consists of a name and a method signature.* Here's an example:

```
delegate bool Filter(string s);
```

This declaration lets you create delegate instances that can hold and invoke methods that return bool and have a single string parameter. In the following example a Filter is created that holds the FirstHalfOfAlphabet method. You then pass the Filter to the Display method, which invokes the Filter:

```
class Test {
  static void Main( ) {
    Filter f = new Filter(FirstHalfOfAlphabet);
    Display(new String [] {"Ant","Lion","Yak"}, f);
  }
  static bool FirstHalfOfAlphabet(string s) {
    return "N".CompareTo(s) > 0;
  }
  static void Display(string[] names, Filter f) {
    int count = 0;
    foreach(string s in names)
      if(f(s)) // invoke delegate
        Console.WriteLine("Item {0} is {1}", count++, s);
  }
}
```

Multicast Delegates

Delegates can hold and invoke multiple methods. In this example, we declare a simple delegate called MethodInvoker, which can hold and then invoke the Foo and Goo methods sequentially. The += method creates a new delegate by adding the right delegate operand to the left delegate operand.

```
using System;
delegate void MethodInvoker( );
class Test {
  static void Main( ) {
    new Test(); // prints "Foo", "Goo"
  }
  Test( ) {
    MethodInvoker m = null;
    m += new MethodInvoker(Foo);
    m += new MethodInvoker(Goo);
    m( );
  }
```

---

* The signature of a delegate method includes its return type and allows the use of a params modifier in its parameter list, expanding the list of elements that characterize an ordinary method signature. The actual name of the target method is irrelevant to the delegate.

```
void Foo( ) {
  Console.WriteLine("Foo");
}
void Goo( ) {
  Console.WriteLine("Goo");
}
}
```

A delegate can also be removed from another delegate using the -= operator:

```
Test( ) {   MethodInvoker m = null;
  m += new MethodInvoker(Foo);
  m -= new MethodInvoker(Foo);
  m( ); // m is now null, throws NullReferenceException
}
```

Delegates are invoked in the order they are added. If a delegate has a non-void return type, then the value of the last delegate invoked is returned. Note that the += and -= operations on a delegate are not thread-safe.

To work with the .NET runtime, C# compiles += and -= operations made on a delegate to the static Combine and Remove methods of the System.Delegate class.

Delegates Compared with Function Pointers

A delegate is behaviorally similar to a C function pointer (or Delphi closure) but can hold multiple methods and the instance associated with each non-static method. In addition, delegates, like all other C# constructs used outside unsafe blocks, are type-safe and secure, which means you're protected from pointing to the wrong type of method or a method that you don't have permission to access.

Delegates Compared with Interfaces

A problem that can be solved with a delegate can also be solved with an interface. For instance, here is how to solve the filter problem using an IFilter interface:

```
using System;
interface IFilter {
  bool Filter(string s);
}
class Test {
  class FirstHalfOfAlphabetFilter : IFilter {
    public bool Filter(string s) {
      return ("N".CompareTo(s) > 0);
    }
  }
```

```
static void Main( ) {
  FirstHalfOfAlphabetFilter f = new FirstHalfOfAlphabetFilter( );
  Display(new string [] {"Ant", "Lion", "Yak"}, f);
}
static void Display(string[] names, IFilter f) {
  int count = 0;
  foreach (string s in names)
    if (f.Filter(s))
      Console.WriteLine("Item {0} is {1}", count++, s);
}
}
```

In this case, the problem was slightly more elegantly handled with a delegate, but generally delegates are best used for event handling.

Events

Event handling is essentially a process by which one object can notify other objects that an event has occurred. This process is largely encapsulated by multicast delegates, which have this ability built in.

Defining a Delegate for an Event

The FCL defines numerous public delegates used for event handling, but you can also write your own. For example:

```
delegate void MoveEventHandler(object source, MoveEventArgs e);
```

By convention, an event delegate's first parameter denotes the source of the event, and the delegate's second parameter derives from System.EventArgs and stores data about the event.

Storing Data for an Event with EventArgs

You can define subclasses of EventArgs to include information relevant to a particular event:

```
public class MoveEventArgs : EventArgs {
  public int newPosition;
  public bool cancel;
  public MoveEventArgs(int newPosition) {
    this.newPosition = newPosition;
  }
}
```

Declaring and Firing an Event

A class or struct can declare an event by applying the event modifier to a delegate field. In this example, the Slider class has a Position property that fires a Move event whenever its Position changes:

```
class Slider {
  int position;
  public event MoveEventHandler Move;
  public int Position {
    get { return position; }
    set {
      if (position != value) { // if position changed
        if (Move != null) { // if invocation list not empty
          MoveEventArgs args = new MoveEventArgs(value);
          Move(this, args); // fire event
          if (args.cancel)
            return;
        }
        position = value;
      }
    }
  }
}
```

The event keyword promotes encapsulation by ensuring that only the += and -= operations can be performed on the delegate. This means other classes can register themselves to be notified of the event, but only the Slider can invoke the delegate (fire the event) or clear the delegate's invocation list.

Acting on an Event with Event Handlers

You can act on an event by adding an event handler to an event. An *event handler* is a delegate that wraps the method you want invoked when the event is fired.

In the next example, we want our Form to act on changes made to a Slider's Position. You do this by creating a MoveEventHandler delegate that wraps the event-handling method, the slider.Move method. This delegate is added to the Move event's existing list of MoveEventHandlers (which starts off empty). Changing the position on the Slider object fires the Move event, which invokes the slider.Move method:

```
class Form {
  static void Main( ) {
    Slider slider = new Slider( );
    // register with the Move event
    slider.Move += new MoveEventHandler(slider_Move);
    slider.Position = 20;
    slider.Position = 60;
```

```
        }
    static void slider_Move(object source, MoveEventArgs e) {
        if(e.newPosition < 50)
            Console.WriteLine("OK");
        else {
            e.cancel = true;
            Console.WriteLine("Can't go that high!");
        }
    }
}
```

Typically, the Slider class would be enhanced to fire the Move event whenever its Position is changed by a mouse movement, keypress, or other user action.

Event Accessors

Syntax:

```
attributes? unsafe? access-modifier?
[
  [[sealed | abstract]? override] |
  new? [virtual | static]?
]?
event delegate type event-property accessor-name
{
    attributes? add statement-block
    attributes? remove statement-block
}
```

Note that abstract accessors don't specify an implementation, so they replace an add/remove block with a semicolon.

Similar to the way properties provide controlled access to a field, event accessors provide controlled access to an event. Consider the following field declaration:

```
public event MoveEventHandler Move;
```

Except for the underscore prefix added to the field (to avoid a name collision), this is semantically identical to:

```
private MoveEventHandler _Move;
public event MoveEventHandler Move {
    add {
        _Move += value;
    }
    remove {
        _Move -= value;
    }
}
```

The ability to specify a custom implementation of add and remove handlers for an event allows a class to proxy an event generated by another class, thus acting as a relay for an event rather than as the generator of that event. Another advantage of this technique is to eliminate the need to store a delegate as a field, which can be costly in terms of storage space. For instance, a class with 100 event fields would store 100 delegate fields, even though maybe only four of those events are actually assigned. Instead, you can store these delegates in a dictionary and add and remove the delegates from that dictionary (assuming the dictionary holding four elements uses less storage space than 100 delegate references).

 The add and remove parts of an event are compiled to add_XXX and remove_XXX methods.

try Statements and Exceptions

Syntax:

```
try statement-block
[catch (exception type value?)? statement-block]+ |
finally statement-block |
[catch (exception type value?)? statement-block]+
finally statement-block
```

try Statement

The purpose of a try statement is to simplify dealing with program execution in exceptional circumstances. A try statement does two things. First, it lets exceptions thrown during the try block's execution be caught by the catch block. Second, it ensures that execution can't leave the try block without first executing the finally block. A try block must be followed by one or more catch blocks, a finally block, or both.

Exceptions

C# *exceptions* are objects that contain information representing the occurrence of an exceptional program state. When an exceptional state has occurred (e.g., a method receives an illegal value), an exception object may be thrown, and the call stack is unwound until the exception is caught by an exception handling block.

In the following example, we have an Account class. An exceptional state for the account class is when its balance is below zero, which occurs when the

Withdraw method receives a withdraw amount larger than the current balance. Our test class makes our customer tiffanyTaylor perform several actions that involve despositing and withdrawing from an account. When she attempts to withdraw more money than she has in her account, a FundException is thrown, which we will catch so we can notify the user and display her current account balance.

```csharp
using System;

public class FundException : Exception {
  public FundException(decimal balance) :
    base("Total funds are "+balance+" dollars") {}
}

class Account {
  decimal balance;
  public decimal Balance {
    get {return balance;}
  }
  public void Deposit(decimal amount) {
    balance += amount;
  }
  public void Withdraw(decimal amount) {
    if (amount > balance)
      throw new FundException(balance);
    balance -= amount;
  }
}

class Customer {
  Account savingsAccount = new Account();
  public void SellBike() {
    savingsAccount.Deposit (1000);
  }
  public void BuyCar() {
    savingsAccount.Withdraw (30000);
  }
  public void GoToMovie() {
    savingsAccount.Withdraw (20);
  }
}

class Test {
  static void Main() {
    Customer tiffanyTaylor = new Customer();
    bool todaysTasksDone = false;
    try {
      tiffanyTaylor.SellBike();
      tiffanyTaylor.BuyCar();
      tiffanyTaylor.GoToMovie();
      todaysTasksDone = true;
    }
```

```
      catch (FundException ex) {
        Console.WriteLine(ex.Message);
      }
      finally {
        Console.WriteLine(todaysTasksDone);
      }
    }
  }
```

At the point when the FundException is thrown, the call stack is comprised of three methods: Withdraw, BuyCar, and Main. Each of these methods will in succession return immediately to its calling method until one of them has a catch block that can handle the exception, in this case Main. Without a try statement, the call stack would have been unwound completely, and our program would have terminated without displaying what caused the problem and without letting the user know whether today's tasks were completed.

catch

A catch clause specifies which exception type (including derived types) to catch. An exception must be of type System.Exception or of a type that derives from System.Exception. Catching System.Exception provides the widest possible net for catching errors, which is useful if your handling of the error is totally generic, such as with an error-logging mechanism. Otherwise, you should catch a more specific exception type to prevent your catch block from dealing with a circumstance it wasn't designed to handle (for example, an out-of-memory exception).

Omitting the exception variable

Specifying only an exception type without a variable name allows an exception to be caught when we don't need to use the exception instance, and merely knowing its type will suffice. The previous example could have been written like this:

```
catch(FundException) { // don't specify variable
  Console.WriteLine("Problem with funds");
}
```

Omitting the catch expression

You may also completely omit the catch expression. This will catch an exception of any type, even types that are not derived from System.Exception (these could be thrown by non–CLS-compliant languages). The previous example could have been written like this:

```
catch {
  Console.WriteLine("Something went wrong...");
}
```

The fact that most exceptions do inherit from System.Exception is a CLS convention, not a CLR requirement.

Specifying multiple catch clauses

When declaring multiple catch clauses, only the first catch clause with an exception type that matches the thrown exception executes its catch block. It is illegal for an exception type B to precede an exception type D if B is a base class of D, since it would be unreachable.

```
try {...}
catch (NullReferenceException) {...}
catch (IOException) {...}
catch {...}
```

finally

finally blocks are always executed when control leaves the try block. A finally block is executed at one of the following times:

- Immediately after the try block completes
- Immediately after the try block prematurely exits with a jump statement (e.g., return, goto) and immediately before the target of the jump statement
- Immediately after a catch block executes

finally blocks add determinism to a program's execution by ensuring that particular code always gets executed.

In our main example, if some other exception occurred such as a memory exception, the finally block would have still been executed. This ensures that the user would know whether today's tasks were completed. The finally block can also be used to gracefully restore program state when an exception occurs. Had our example used a connection to a remote account object, it would have been appropriate to close the account in the finally block.

Key Properties of the System.Exception Class

You will most frequently use the following properties of System.Exception:

StackTrace
> This is a string representing all the methods called from the origin of the exception to the catch block.

Message

This is a string with a description of the error.

InnerException

Sometimes it is useful to catch an exception, then throw a new, more specific exception. For instance, you can catch an IOException, and then throw a DocumentLoadException that contains more specific information on what went wrong. In this scenario, the DocumentLoadException should include the IOException as the InnerException argument in its constructor, which is assigned to the InnerException property. This cascading exception structure can be particularly useful for debugging.

 In C# all exceptions are runtime exceptions; there is no equivalent of Java's compile-time exceptions.

Attributes

Syntax:
```
[[target:]? attribute-name (
positional-param+ |
[named-param = expression]+ |
positional-param+, [named-param = expression]+)?]
```

Attributes are language constructs that can decorate code elements (e.g., assemblies, modules, types, members, return values, and parameters) with additional information.

In every language, you specify information associated with the types, methods, parameters, and other elements of your program. For example, a type can specify a list of interfaces that it derives from, or a parameter can specify how its values are to be passed with modifiers such as the ref modifier in C#. The limitation of this approach is that you can only associate information with code elements using the predefined constructs that the language itself provides.

Attributes allow programmers to add to the types of information associated with these code elements. For example, serialization in the .NET Framework uses various serialization attributes applied to types and fields to define how these code elements are serialized. This is more flexible than requiring the language to have special syntax for serialization.

Attribute Classes

An attribute is defined by a class that inherits (directly or indirectly) from the abstract class System.Attribute. When specifying an attribute on an element, the attribute name is the name of the type. By convention the derived type name ends with the word "Attribute", but this suffix isn't required.

In this example we specify that the Foo class is serializable using the Serializable attribute:

```
[Serializable]
public class Foo {...}
```

The Serializable attribute is actually a type declared in the System namespace, as follows:

```
class SerializableAttribute : Attribute {...}
```

We could also specify the Serializable attribute using its fully qualified typename, as follows:

```
[System.SerializableAttribute]
public class Foo {...}
```

The preceding two examples that use the Serializable attribute are semantically identical.

 The C# language and the FCL include a number of predefined attributes. For more information on the other attributes included in the FCL, and on creating your own attributes, see "Custom Attributes" in Chapter 3.

Named and Positional Parameters

Attributes can take parameters, which specify additional information on the code element beyond the mere presence of the attribute.

In this next example, we use the WebPermission attribute to specify that methods in class Foo cannot make web connections to any URL starting with *http://www.oreilly.com/*. This attribute allows you to include parameters that specify a security action and a URL:

```
[WebPermission(SecurityAction.Deny,
    ConnectPattern="http://www.oreilly.com/.*")]
public class Foo {...}
```

Attribute parameters fall into one of two categories: positional and named parameters. In the preceding example, SecurityAction.Deny is a positional parameter, and ConnectPattern="http://www.oreilly.com/.*" is a named parameter.

The positional parameters for an attribute correspond to the parameters passed to one of the attribute type's public constructors. The named parameters for an attribute correspond to the set of public read/write or write-only instance properties and fields on the attribute type.

Since the parameters used when specifying an attribute are evaluated at compile time, they are generally limited to constant expressions.

Explicitly Specifying Attribute Targets

Implicitly, the target of an attribute is the code element it immediately precedes. However, sometimes it is necessary to explicitly specify that the attribute applies to a particular target. The possible targets are assembly, module, type, method, property, field, param, event, and return.

Here is an example that uses the CLSCompliant attribute to specify the level of CLS compliance for an entire assembly:

```
[assembly:CLSCompliant(true)]
```

Specifying Multiple Attributes

You can specify multiple attributes on a single code element. Each attribute can be listed within the same pair of square brackets (separated by a comma), in separate pairs of square brackets, or any combination of the two.

Consequently, the following three examples are semantically identical:

```
[Serializable, Obsolete, CLSCompliant(false)]
public class Bar {...}

[Serializable]
[Obsolete]
[CLSCompliant(false)]
public class Bar {...}

[Serializable, Obsolete]
[CLSCompliant(false)]
public class Bar {...}
```

Unsafe Code and Pointers

C# supports direct memory manipulation via pointers within blocks of code marked unsafe and compiled with the /unsafe compiler option. Pointer types are primarily useful for interoperability with C APIs but may also be used for accessing memory outside the managed heap or for performance-critical hotspots.

Pointer Types

For every value type or pointer type V in a C# program, there is a corresponding C# pointer type named V*. A pointer instance holds the address of a value. That value is considered to be of type V, but pointer types can be (unsafely) cast to any other pointer type. Table 2-3 summarizes the principal pointer operators supported by the C# language.

Table 2-3. Principal pointer operators

Operator	Meaning
&	The *address-of* operator returns a pointer to the address of a value.
*	The *dereference* operator returns the value at the address of a pointer.
->	The *pointer-to-member* operator is a syntactic shortcut, in which x->y is equivalent to (*x).y.

Unsafe Code

By marking a type, type-member, or statement block with the unsafe keyword, you're permitted to use pointer types and perform C++-style pointer operations on memory within that scope. Here is an example that uses pointers with a managed object:

```
unsafe void RedFilter(int[,] bitmap) {
  const int length = bitmap.Length;
  fixed (int* b = bitmap) {
    int* p = b;
    for(int i = 0; i < length; i++)
      *p++ &= 0xFF;
  }
}
```

Unsafe code typically runs faster than a corresponding safe implementation, which in this case would have required a nested loop with array indexing and bounds checking. An unsafe C# method can be faster than calling an external C function too, since there is no overhead associated with leaving the managed execution environment.

The fixed Statement

Syntax:

```
fixed ([value type | void ]* name = [&]? expression )
 statement-block
```

The fixed statement is required to pin a managed object, such as the bitmap in the previous pointer example. During the execution of a program, many objects are allocated and deallocated from the heap. In order to avoid the unnecessary waste or fragmentation of memory, the garbage collector moves objects around. Pointing to an object would be futile if its address can change while referencing it, so the fixed statement tells the garbage collector to pin the object and not move it around. This can impact the efficiency of the runtime, so fixed blocks should be used only briefly, and preferably, heap allocation should be avoided within the fixed block.

C# returns a pointer only from a value type, never directly from a reference type. Arrays and strings are an exception to this, but only syntactically, since they actually return a pointer to their first element (which must be a value type), rather than the objects themselves.

Value types declared inline within reference types require the reference type to be pinned, as follows:

```csharp
using System;
class Test {
  int x;
  static void Main() {
    Test test = new Test();
    unsafe {
        fixed(int* p = &test.x) { // pins Test
          *p = 9;
        }
        System.Console.WriteLine(test.x);
    }
  }
}
```

Pointer to Member Operator

In addition to the & and * operators, C# also provides the C++-style -> operator, which can be used on structs:

```csharp
using System;
struct Test {
    int x;
    unsafe static void Main() {
        Test test = new Test();
        Test* p = &test;
```

```
        p->x = 9;
        System.Console.WriteLine(test.x);
    }
}
```

The stackalloc Keyword

Memory can be allocated in a block on the stack explicitly using the stackalloc keyword. Since it is allocated on the stack, its lifetime is limited to the execution of the method in which it is used, just as with other local variables. The block may use [ ] indexing but is purely a value type with no additional self-describing information or bounds checking, which an array provides:

```
int* a = stackalloc int [10];
for (int i = 0; i < 10; ++i)
    Console.WriteLine(a[i]); // print raw memory
```

void*

Rather than pointing to a specific value type, a pointer may make no assumptions about the type of the underlying data. This is useful for functions that deal with raw memory. An implicit conversion exists from any pointer type to a void*. A void* cannot be dereferenced, and arithmetic operations cannot be performed on void pointers. For example:

```
class Test {
  unsafe static void Main ( ) {
    short[ ] a = {1,1,2,3,5,8,13,21,34,55};
      fixed (short* p = a) {
        // sizeof returns size of value-type in bytes
        Zap (p, a.Length * sizeof (short));
      }
    foreach (short x in a)
      System.Console.WriteLine (x); // prints all zeros
  }
  unsafe static void Zap (void* memory, int byteCount) {
    byte* b = (byte*)memory;
      for (int i = 0; i < byteCount; i++)
        *b++ = 0;
  }
}
```

Pointers to Unmanaged Code

Pointers are also useful for accessing data outside the managed heap, such as when interacting with C DLLs or COM or when dealing with data not in the main memory, such as graphics memory or a storage medium on an embedded device.

Preprocessor Directives

Preprocessor directives supply the compiler with additional information about regions of code. The most common preprocessor directives are the conditional directives, which provide a way to include or exclude regions of code from compilation. For example:

```
#define DEBUG
using System;
class MyClass {
  int x;
  public void Foo() {
  # if DEBUG
  # warning "Debug mode is ON"
    Console.WriteLine("Testing: x = {0}", x);
  # endif
  }
}
```

In this class, the statement in Foo is compiled conditionally, dependent upon the presence of the user-selected DEBUG symbol. If you remove the DEBUG symbol, the statement isn't compiled. Preprocessor symbols can be defined within a source file as just shown and can be passed to the compiler with the /define:symbol command-line option.

The #error and #warning symbols prevent accidental misuse of conditional directives by making the compiler generate a warning or error given an undesirable set of compilation symbols.

Preprocessor Directives

The C# language supports the preprocessor directives shown in Table 2-4.

Table 2-4. Preprocessor directives

Preprocessor directive	Action
#define symbol	Defines symbol
#undef symbol	Undefines symbol
#if symbol [operator symbol2] ...	symbol to test; operator: ==, !=, &&, || followed by #else, #elif, #endif
#else	Executes code to subsequent #endif
#elif symbol [operator symbol2]	Combines #else branch and #if test

Table 2-4. Preprocessor directives (continued)

Preprocessor directive	Action
#endif	Ends conditional directives
#warning *text*	*text*: warning text to appear in compiler output
#error *text*	*text*: error message to appear in compiler output
#line *number* [*file*]	*number* specifies line in source code; *file* is the filename to appear in computer output
#region *name*	Marks beginning of outline
#end *region*	Ends an outline region

XML Documentation

C# offers three different styles of source code documentation: single-line comments, multiline comments, and documentation comments.

C/C++-Style Comments

Single- and multiline comments use the C++ syntax: // and /*...*/:

```
int x = 3; // this is a comment
MyMethod( ); /* this is a
comment that spans two lines */
```

The disadvantage of this style of commenting is that there is no predetermined standard for documenting your types. Consequently, it can't be easily parsed to automate the production of documentation. C# improves on this by allowing you to embed documentation comments in the source and by providing an automated mechanism for extracting and validating documentation at compile time.

Documentation Comments

Documentation comments are similar to C# single-line comments but start with /// and can be applied to any user-defined type or member. These comments can include embedded XML tags as well as descriptive text. These tags allow you to mark up the descriptive text to better define the semantics of the type or member and also to incorporate cross-references.

These comments can then be extracted at compile time into a separate output file containing the documentation. The compiler validates the comments for internal consistency, expands cross-references into fully qualified type IDs, and outputs a well-formed XML file. Further processing is left up to you, although a common next step is to run the XML through an XSL/T, generating HTML documentation.

Here is an example documentation for a simple type:

```
// Filename: DocTest.cs
using System;
class MyClass {
  /// <summary>
  /// The Foo method is called from
  ///    <see cref="Main">Main</see>
  /// </summary>
  /// <mytag>Secret stuff</mytag>
  /// <param name="s">Description for s</param>
  static void Foo(string s) { Console.WriteLine(s); }
  static void Main() { Foo("42"); }
}
```

XML Documentation Files

When the preceding source file is run through the compiler with the /doc:
<*filename*> command-line options, this XML file is generated:

```
<?xml version="1.0"?>
<doc>
  <assembly>
    <name>DocTest</name>
  </assembly>
  <members>
    <member name="M:MyClass.Foo(System.String)">
      <summary>
      The Foo method is called from
        <see cref="M:MyClass.Main">Main</see>
      </summary>
      <mytag>Secret stuff</mytag>
      <param name="s">Description for s</param>
    </member>
  </members>
</doc>
```

The <?xml...>, <doc>, and <members> tags are generated automatically and
form the skeleton for the XML file. The <assembly> and <name> tags indicate
the assembly that this type lives in. Every member preceded by a documentation comment is included in the XML file via a <member> tag with a name
attribute that identifies the member. Note that the cref attribute in the <see>
tag has also been expanded to refer to a fully qualified type and member.
The predefined XML documentation tags embedded in the documentation
comments are also included in the XML file. The tags have been validated to
ensure that all parameters are documented, that the names are accurate, and
that any cross-references to other types or members can be resolved. Finally,
any additional user-defined tags are transferred verbatim.

Predefined XML Tags

This section lists the predefined set of XML tags that can be used to mark up the descriptive text:

`<summary>`, `<remarks>`

```
<summary>description</summary>
<remarks>description</remarks>
```

These tags describe a type or member. Typically, `<summary>` contains the description of a member, and `<remarks>` contains a full description of a type.

`<param>`

```
<param name="name">description</param>
```

This tag describes a parameter on a method. The *name* attribute is mandatory and must refer to a parameter on the method. If this tag is applied to any parameter on a method, all parameters on that method must be documented. You must enclose *name* in double quotation marks ("").

`<returns>`

```
<returns>description</returns>
```

This tag describes the return values for a method.

`<exception>`

```
<exception [cref="type"]>description</exception>
```

This tag describes the exceptions a method may throw. If present, the optional `cref` attribute should refer to the type of exception. You must enclose the type name in double quotation marks ("").

`<permission>`

```
<permission [cref="type"]>description</permission>
```

This tag describes the permission requirements for a type or member. If present, the optional `cref` attribute should refer to the type that represents the permission set required by the member, although the compiler doesn't validate this. You must enclose the type name in double quotation marks ("").

`<example>`, `<c>`, `<code>`

```
<example>description</example>
<c>code</c>
<code>code</code>
```

These tags provide a description and sample source code explaining the use of a type or member. Typically, the `<example>` tag provides the description and contains the `<c>` and `<code>` tags, although these can also be used independently. If you need to include an inline code snippet, use the `<c>` tag. If you need to include multiline snippets, use the `<code>` tag.

`<see>, <seealso>`

```
<see cref="member">text</see>
<seealso cref="member">text</seealso>
```

These tags identify cross-references in the documentation to other types or members. Typically, the `<see>` tag is used inline within a description, while the `<seealso>` tag is broken out into a separate "See Also" section. These tags are useful because they allow tools to generate cross-references, indexes, and hyperlinked views of the documentation. Member names must be enclosed by double quotation marks ("").

`<value>`

```
<value>description</value>
```

This tag describes a property on a class.

`<paramref>`

```
<paramref name="name"/>
```

This tag identifies the use of a parameter name within descriptive text, such as `<remarks>` or `<summary>`. The name must be enclosed by double quotation marks ("").

`<list>, <para>`

```
<list type=[bullet|number|table]>
 <listheader>
 <term>name</term>
 <description>description</description>
 </listheader>
 <item>
 <term>name</term>
 <description>description</description>
 </item>
</list>
<para>text</para>
```

These tags provide hints to documentation generators on how to format the documentation.

`<include>`

```
<include file='filename' path='path-to-element'>
```

This tag specirfies an external file that contains documentation and an XPath path to a specific element in that file. For example, a path of docs[@id="001"]/* would retrieve whatever is inside of `<docs id="001"/>`. The filename and path must be enclosed by single quotation marks (' ').

User-Defined Tags

There is little that is special about the predefined XML tags recognized by the C# compiler, and you are free to define your own. The only special processing done by the compiler is on the `<param>` tag (where it verifies the parameter name and confirms that all the parameters on the method are documented) and the `cref` attribute (where it verifies that the attribute refers to a real type or member and expands it to a fully qualified type or member ID). The `cref` attribute can also be used in your own tags and is verified and expanded just as it is in the predefined <exception>, <permission>, <see>, and <seealso> tags.

Type or Member Cross-References

Type names and type or member cross-references are translated into IDs that uniquely define the type or member. These names are composed of a prefix that defines what the ID represents and a signature of the type or member. Table 2-5 lists the set of type and member prefixes.

Table 2-5. XML type ID prefixes

Prefix	Applied to
N	Namespace
T	Type (class, struct, enum, interface, delegate)
F	Field
P	Property (includes indexers)
M	Method (includes special methods)
E	Event
!	Error

The rules describing how the signatures are generated are well-documented, although fairly complex.

Here is an example of a type and the IDs that are generated:

```
// Namespaces do not have independent signatures
namespace NS {
  // T:NS.MyClass
  class MyClass {
    // F:NS.MyClass.aField
    string aField;
    // P:NS.MyClass.aProperty
    short aProperty {get {...} set {...}}
    // T:NS.MyClass.NestedType
    class NestedType {...};
    // M:NS.MyClass.X()
    void X() {...}
    // M:NS.MyClass.Y(System.Int32,System.Double@,System.Decimal@)
    void Y(int p1, ref double p2, out decimal p3) {...}
    // M:NS.MyClass.Z(System.Char[],System.Single[0:,0:])
    void Z(char[] p1, float[,] p2) {...}
    // M:NS.MyClass.op_Addition(NS.MyClass,NS.MyClass)
```

```
    public static MyClass operator+(MyClass c1, MyClass c2) {...}
    // M:NS.MyClass.op_Implicit(NS.MyClass)~System.Int32
    public static implicit operator int(MyClass c) {...}
    // M:NS.MyClass.#ctor
    MyClass() {...}
    // M:NS.MyClass.Finalize
    ~MyClass() {...}
    // M:NS.MyClass.#cctor
    static MyClass() {...}
  }
}
```

CHAPTER 3
Programming the
.NET Framework

Most modern programming languages include some form of runtime that provides common services and access to the underlying operating systems and hardware. Examples of this range from a simple functional library, such as the ANSI C Runtime used by C and C++, to the rich object-oriented class libraries provided by the Java Runtime Environment.

Similar to the way that Java programs depend on the Java class libraries and virtual machine, C# programs depend on the services in the .NET Framework such as the framework class library (FCL) and the Common Language Runtime (CLR).

For a high-level overview of the FCL, see Chapter 4.

This chapter addresses the most common tasks you need to perform when building C# programs. These topics generally fall into one of two categories: leveraging functionality included in the FCL and interacting with elements of the CLR.

Common Types

Certain types in the FCL are ubiquitous, in that they are fundamental to the way the FCL and CLR work and provide common functionality used throughout the entire FCL.

This section identifies some of the most common of these types and provides guidelines to their usage. The types mentioned in this section all exist in the System namespace.

Object Class

The System.Object class is the root of the class hierarchy and serves as the base class for every other class. The C# object type aliases System.Object. System.Object provides a handful of useful methods that are present on all objects, and whose signatures are listed in the following fragment of the System.Object class definition:

```
public class Object {
    public Object( ) {...}
    public virtual bool Equals(object o) {...}
    public virtual int GetHashCode( ){...}
    public Type GetType( ){...}
    public virtual string ToString( ) {...}
    protected virtual void Finalize( ) {...}
    protected object MemberwiseClone( ) {...}
    public static bool Equals (object a, object b) {...}
    public static bool ReferenceEquals (object a, object b) {...}
}
```

Object( )

> The constructor for the Object base class.

Equals(object o)

> This method evaluates whether two objects are equivalent.

> The default implementation of this method compares the objects by reference, so classes are expected to override this method to compare two objects by value.

> In C#, you can also overload the == and != operators. For more information see "Implementing value equality" in the "Classes and Structs" section in Chapter 2.

GetHashCode( )

> This method allows types to hash their instances. A hashcode is an integer value that provides a "pretty good" unique ID for an object. If two objects hash to the same value, there's a good chance that they are also equal. If they don't hash to the same value, they are definitely not equal.

> The hashcode is used when you store a key in a dictionary or hashtable collection, but you can also use it to optimize Equals( ) by comparing hash codes and skipping comparisons of values that are obviously not equal. This is a gain only when it is cheaper to create the hashcode than perform an equality comparison. If your hashcode is based on immutable data members, you can make this a no-brainer by caching the hash code the first time it is computed.

> The return value from this function should pass the following tests: (1) two objects representing the same value should return the same hash-

code, and (2) the returned values should generate a random distribution at runtime.

The default implementation of GetHashCode doesn't actually meet these criteria because it merely returns a number based on the object reference. For this reason, you should usually override this method in your own types.

An implementation of GetHashCode could simply add or multiply all the data members together. You can achieve a more random distribution of hash codes by combining each member with a prime number (see Example 3-1).

To learn more about how the hashcode is used by the predefined collection classes, see "Collections" later in this chapter.

GetType( )

This method provides access to the Type object representing the type of the object and should never be implemented by your types. To learn more about the Type object and reflection in general, see the later section "Reflection."

ToString( )

This method provides a string representation of the object and is generally intended for use when debugging or producing human-readable output.

The default implementation of this method merely returns the name of the type and should be overridden in your own types to return a meaningful string representation of the object. The predefined types such as int and string all override this method to return the value, as follows:

```
using System;
class Beeblebrox {}
class Test {
  static void Main( ) {
    string s = "Zaphod";
    Beeblebrox b = new Beeblebrox( );
    Console.WriteLine(s); // Prints "Zaphod"
    Console.WriteLine(b); // Prints "Beeblebrox"
  }
}
```

Finalize( )

The Finalize method cleans up nonmemory resources and is usually called by the garbage collector before reclaiming the memory for the object. The Finalize method can be overridden on any reference type, but this should be done only in a very few cases. For a discussion of finalizers and the garbage collector, see the later section "Automatic Memory Management."

MemberwiseClone( )

This method creates shallow copies of the object and should never be implemented by your types. To learn how to control shallow/deep copy semantics on your own types, see "ICloneable Interface" later in this chapter

Equals/ReferenceEquals (object *a*, object *b*)

Equals tests for value quality, and ReferenceEquals tests for reference equality. Equals basically calls the instance Equals method on the first object, using the second object as a parameter. In the case that both object references are null, it returns true, and in the case that only one reference is null, it returns false. The ReferenceEquals method returns true if both object references point to the same object or if both object references are null.

Creating FCL-friendly types

When defining new types that work well with the rest of the FCL, you should override several of these methods as appropriate.

Example 3-1 is an example of a new value type that is intended to be a good citizen in the FCL:

Example 3-1. Defining new value type

```
// Point3D - a 3D point
// Compile with: csc /t:library Point3D.cs
using System;
public sealed class Point3D {
  int x, y, z;
  public Point3D(int x, int y, int z) {
    this.x=x; this.y=y; this.z=z; // Initialize data
  }
  public override bool Equals(object o) {
    if (o == (object) this) return true; // Identity test
    if (o == null) return false; // Safety test
    if (!(o is Point3D)) // Type equivalence test
      return false;
    Point3D p = (Point3D) o;
    return ((this.x==p.x) && (this.y==p.y) && (this.z==p.z));
  }
  public override int GetHashCode(){
    return ((((37+x)*37)+y)*37)+z; // :-)
  }
  public override string ToString() {
    return String.Format("[{0},{1},{2}]", x, y, z);
  }
}
```

This class overrides Equals to provide value-based equality semantics, creates a hashcode that follows the rules described in the preceding section, and overrides ToString for easy debugging. It can be used as follows:

```
// TestPoint3D - test the 3D point type
// Compile with: csc /r:Point3D.dll TestPoint3D.cs
using System;
using System.Collections;
class TestPoint3D {
  static void Main() {
    // Uses ToString, prints "p1=[1,1,1] p2=[2,2,2] p3=[2,2,2]"
    Point3D p1 = new Point3D(1,1,1);
    Point3D p2 = new Point3D(2,2,2);
    Point3D p3 = new Point3D(2,2,2);
    Console.WriteLine("p1={0} p2={1} p3={2}", p1, p2, p3);

    // Tests for equality to demonstrate Equals
    Console.WriteLine(Equals(p1, p2)); // Prints "False"
    Console.WriteLine(Equals(p2, p3)); // Prints "True"

    // Use a hashtable to cache each point's variable name
    // (uses GetHashCode).
    Hashtable ht = new Hashtable();
    ht[p1] = "p1";
    ht[p2] = "p2";
    ht[p3] = "p3"; // replaces ht[p2], since p2 == p3

    // Prints:
    //    p1 is at [1,1,1]
    //    p3 is at [2,2,2]
    foreach (DictionaryEntry de in ht)
      Console.WriteLine("{0} is at {1} ", de.Value, de.Key);
  }
}
```

ICloneable Interface

```
public interface ICloneable {
  object Clone();
}
```

ICloneable allows class or struct instances to be cloned. It contains a single method named Clone that returns a copy of the instance. When implementing this interface your Clone method can simply return this. MemberwiseClone(), which performs a shallow copy (the fields are copied directly), or you can perform a custom deep copy, in which you clone individual fields in the class or struct. The following example is the simplest implementation of ICloneable:

```
public class Foo : ICloneable {
    public object Clone() {
```

```
      return this.MemberwiseClone( );
  }
}
```

IComparable Interface

```
interface IComparable {
  int CompareTo(object o);
}
```

IComparable is implemented by types that have instances that can be ordered (see the later section "Collections"). It contains a single method named CompareTo that:

- Returns - if instance < o
- Returns + if instance > o
- Returns 0 if instance == o

This interface is implemented by all numeric types: string, DateTime, etc. It may also be implemented by custom classes or structs to provide comparison semantics. For example:

```
using System;
using System.Collections;
class MyType : IComparable {
  public int x;
  public MyType(int x) {
    this.x = x;
  }
  public int CompareTo(object o) {
    return x -((MyType)o).x;
  }
}
class Test {
  static void Main( ) {
    ArrayList a = new ArrayList( );
    a.Add(new MyType(42));
    a.Add(new MyType(17));
    a.Sort( );
    foreach(MyType t in a)
      Console.WriteLine(((MyType)t).x);
  }
}
```

IFormattable Interface

```
public interface IFormattable {
  string ToString(string format, IFormatProvider formatProvider);
}
```

The IFormattable interface is implemented by types that have formatting options for converting their value to a string representation. For instance, a decimal may be converted to a string representing currency or to a string that uses a comma for a decimal point. The formatting options are specified by the *format string* (see "Formatting Strings" later in this chapter). If an IFormatProvider interface is supplied, it specifies the specific culture to be used for the conversion.

IFormattable is commonly used when calling one of the String class Format methods (see the later section "Strings").

All the common types (int, string, DateTime, etc.) implement this interface, and you should implement it on your own types if you want them to be fully supported by the String class when formatting.

Math

C# and the FCL provide a rich set of features that make math-oriented programming easy and efficient.

This section identifies some of the most common types applicable to math programming and demonstrates how to build new math types. The types mentioned in this section exist in the System namespace.

Language Support for Math

C# has many useful features for math and can even build custom mathematical types. Operator overloading allows custom mathematical types, such as complex numbers and vectors, to be used in a natural way. Rectangular arrays provide a fast and easy way to express matrices. Finally, structs allow the efficient creation of low-overhead objects. For example:

```
struct Vector {
  float direction;
  float magnitude;
  public Vector(float direction, float magnitude) {
    this.direction = direction;
    this.magnitude = magnitude;
  }
  public static Vector operator *(Vector v, float scale) {
    return new Vector(v.direction, v.magnitude * scale);
  }
  public static Vector operator /(Vector v, float scale) {
    return new Vector(v.direction, v.magnitude * scale);
  }
  // ...
}
class Test {
```

```
      static void Main( ) {
      Vector [,] matrix = {{new Vector(1f,2f), new Vector(6f,2f)},
                            {new Vector(7f,3f), new Vector(4f,9f)}};
      for (int i=0; i<matrix.GetLength(0); i++)
        for (int j=0; j<matrix.GetLength(1); j++)
          matrix[i, j] *= 2f;
      }
    }
```

Special Types and Operators

The decimal datatype is useful for financial calculations, since it is a base10 number that can store 28 to 29 significant figures (see "decimal type" in the "Types" section in Chapter 2).

The checked operator allows integral operations to be bounds checked (see "Arithmetic Overflow Check Operators" in the "Expressions and Operators" section in Chapter 2).

Math Class

The Math class provides static methods and constants for basic mathematical purposes. All trigonometric and exponential functions use the double type, and all angles use radians. For example:

```
using System;
class Test {
  static void Main( ) {
    double a = 3;
    double b = 4;
    double C = Math.PI / 2;
    double c = Math.Sqrt (a*a+b*b-2*a*b*Math.Cos(C));
    Console.WriteLine("The length of side c is "+c);
  }
}
```

Random Class

The Random class produces pseudo-random numbers and may be extended if you require greater randomness (for cryptographically strong random numbers, see the System.Security.Cryptography.RandomNumberGenerator class). The random values returned are always between a minimum (inclusive) value and a maximum (exclusive) value. By default, the Random class uses the current time as its seed, but a custom seed can also be supplied to the constructor. Here's a simple example:

```
Random r = new Random( );
Console.WriteLine(r.Next(50)); // return between 0 and 50
```

Strings

C# offers a wide range of string-handling features. Support is provided for both mutable and immutable strings, extensible string formatting, locale-aware string comparisons, and multiple string encoding systems.

This section introduces and demonstrates the most common types you'll use when working with strings. Unless otherwise stated, the types mentioned in this section all exist in the System or System.Text namespaces.

String Class

A C# string represents an immutable sequence of characters and aliases the System.String class. Strings have comparison, appending, inserting, conversion, copying, formatting, indexing, joining, splitting, padding, trimming, removing, replacing, and searching methods. The compiler converts + operations on operands where the left operand is a string to Concat methods and preevaluates and interns string constants wherever possible.

Immutability of Strings

Strings are immutable, which means they can't be modified after creation. Consequently, many of the methods that initially appear to modify a string actually create a new string:

```
string a = "Heat";
string b = a.Insert(3, "r");
Console.WriteLine(b); // Prints Heart
```

If you need a mutable string, see the StringBuilder class.

String Interning

In addition, the immutability of strings enable all strings in an application to be interned. *Interning* describes the process whereby all the constant strings in an application are stored in a common place, and any duplicate strings are eliminated. This saves space at runtime but creates the possibility that multiple string references will point at the same spot in memory. This can be the source of unexpected results when comparing two constant strings, as follows:

```
string a = "hello";
string b = "hello";
Console.WriteLine(a == b); // True for String only
Console.WriteLine(a.Equals(b)); // True for all objects
Console.WriteLine(Object.ReferenceEquals(a, b)); // True!!
```

Formatting Strings

The Format method provides a convenient way to build strings that embed string representations of a variable number of parameters. Each parameter can be of any type, including both predefined types and user-defined types.

The Format method takes a format-specification string and a variable number of parameters. The format-specification string defines the template for the string and includes format specifications for each of the parameters. The syntax of a format specifier looks like this:

```
{ParamIndex[,MinWidth][:FormatString]}
```

ParamIndex

The zero-based index of the parameter to be formatted.

MinWidth

The minimum number of characters for the string representation of the parameter, to be padded by spaces if necessary (negative is left-justified, positive is right-justified).

FormatString

If the parameter represents an object that implements IFormattable, the FormatString is passed to the ToString method on IFormattable to construct the string. If not, the ToString method on Object is used to construct the string.

 All of the common types (int, string, DateTime, etc.) implement IFormattable. A table of the numeric and picture format specifiers supported by the common predefined types is provided in Appendix C.

In the following example, we embed a basic string representation of the account variable (param 0) and a monetary string representation of the cash variable (param 1, C=Currency):

```
using System;
class TestFormatting {
  static void Main( ) {
    int i = 2;
    decimal m = 42.73m;
    string s = String.Format("Account {0} has {1:C}.", i, m);
    Console.WriteLine(s); // Prints "Account 2 has $42.73"
  }
}
```

Indexing Strings

Consistent with all other indexing in the CLR, the characters in a string are accessed with a zero-based index:

```
using System;
class TestIndexing {
  static void Main( ) {
    string s = "Going down?";
    for (int i=0; i<s.Length; i++)
      Console.WriteLine(s[i]); // Prints s vertically
  }
}
```

Encoding Strings

Strings can be converted between different character encodings using the Encoding type. The Encoding type can't be created directly, but the ASCII, Unicode, UTF7, UTF8, and BigEndianUnicode static properties on the Encoding type return correctly constructed instances.

Here is an example that converts an array of bytes into a string using the ASCII encoding:

```
using System;
using System.Text;
class TestEncoding {
  static void Main( ) {
    byte[] ba = new byte[] { 67, 35, 32, 105, 115,
                             32, 67, 79, 79, 76, 33 };
    string s = Encoding.ASCII.GetString(ba);
    Console.WriteLine(s);
  }
}
```

StringBuilder Class

The StringBuilder class is used to represent mutable strings. It starts at a predefined size (16 characters by default) and grows dynamically as more string data is added. It can either grow unbounded or up to a configurable maximum. For example:

```
using System;
using System.Text;
class TestStringBuilder {
  static void Main( ) {
    StringBuilder sb = new StringBuilder("Hello, ");
    sb.Append("World?");
    sb[12] = '!';
```

```
    Console.WriteLine(sb); // Hello, World!
  }
}
```

Collections

Collections are standard data structures that supplement arrays, the only
built-in data structures in C#. This differs from languages such as Perl and
Python, which incorporate key-value data structures and dynamically sized
arrays into the language itself.

The FCL includes a set of types that provide commonly required data structures and support for creating your own. These types are typically broken
down into two categories: *interfaces* that define a standardized set of design
patterns for collection classes in general, and concrete *classes* that implement these interfaces and provide a usable range of data structures.

This section introduces all the concrete collection classes and abstract collection interfaces and provides examples of their use. Unless otherwise
stated, the types mentioned in this section all exist in the System.Col-
lections namespace.

Concrete Collection Classes

The FCL includes the concrete implementations of the collection design patterns that are described in this section.

Unlike C++, C# doesn't yet support templates, so these implementations
work generically by accepting elements of type System.Object.

ArrayList class

ArrayList is a dynamically sized array of objects that implements the IList
interface (see "IList interface" later in this chapter). An ArrayList works by
maintaining an internal array of objects that is replaced with a larger array
when it reaches its capacity of elements. It is very efficient at adding elements (since there is usually a free slot at the end) but is inefficient at inserting elements (since all elements have to be shifted to make a free slot).
Searching can be efficient if the BinarySearch method is used, but you must
Sort() the ArrayList first. You could use the Contains() method, but it performs a linear search in O(n) time.

```
ArrayList a = new ArrayList();
a.Add("Vernon");
a.Add("Corey");
a.Add("William");
```

```
a.Add("Muzz");
a.Sort( );
for(int i = 0; i < a.Count; i++)
   Console.WriteLine(a [i]);
```

BitArray class

A `BitArray` is a dynamically sized array of Boolean values. It is more memory-efficient than a simple array of `bool`s because it uses only one bit for each value, whereas a `bool` array uses two bytes for each value. Here is an example of its use:

```
BitArray bits = new BitArray(0); // initialize a zero-length bit array
bits.Length = 2;
bits[1] = true;
bits.Xor(bits); // Xor the array with itself
```

Hashtable class

A `Hashtable` is a standard dictionary (key/value) data structure that uses a hashing algorithm to store and index values efficiently. This hashing algorithm is performed using the hashcode returned by the `GetHashCode` method on `System.Object`. Types used as keys in a `Hashtable` should therefore override `GetHashCode` to return a good hash of the object's internal value.

```
Hashtable ht = new Hashtable( );
ht["One"] = 1;
ht["Two"] = 2;
ht["Three"] = 3;
Console.WriteLine(ht["Two"]); // Prints "2"
```

`Hashtable` also implements `IDictionary` (see "IDictionary interface" later in this chapter), and therefore, can be manipulated as a normal dictionary data structure.

Queue class

A `Queue` is a standard first-in, first-out (FIFO) data structure, providing simple operations to enqueue, dequeue, peek, etc. Here is an example:

```
Queue q = new Queue( );
q.Enqueue(1);
q.Enqueue(2);
Console.WriteLine(q.Dequeue( )); // Prints "1"
Console.WriteLine(q.Dequeue( )); // Prints "2"
```

SortedList class

A `SortedList` is a standard dictionary data structure that uses a binary-chop search to index efficiently. `SortedList` implements `IDictionary` (see the later section "IDictionary interface"):

```
SortedList s = new SortedList( );
s["Zebra"] = 1;
s["Antelope"] = 2;
s["Eland"] = 3;
s["Giraffe"] = 4;
s["Meerkat"] = 5;
s["Dassie"] = 6;
s["Tokoloshe"] = 7;
Console.WriteLine(s["Meerkat"]); // Prints "5" in 3 lookups
```

Stack class

A Stack is a standard last-in first-out (LIFO) data structure:

```
Stack s = new Stack( );
s.Push(1); // Stack = 1
s.Push(2); // Stack = 1,2
s.Push(3); // Stack = 1,2,3
Console.WriteLine(s.Pop( )); // Prints 3, Stack=1,2
Console.WriteLine(s.Pop( )); // Prints 2, Stack=1
Console.WriteLine(s.Pop( )); // Prints 1, Stack=
```

StringCollection class

A StringCollection is a standard collection data structure for storing strings. StringCollection lives in the System.Collections.Specialized namespace and implements ICollection. It can be manipulated like a normal collection (see the later section "ICollection interface"):

```
StringCollection sc = new StringCollection( );
sc.Add("s1");
string[] sarr = {"s2", "s3", "s4"};
sc.AddRange(sarr);
foreach (string s in sc)
  Console.Write("{0} ", s); // s1 s2 s3 s4
```

Collection Interfaces

The collection interfaces provide standard ways to enumerate, populate, and author collections. The FCL defines the interfaces in this section to support the standard collection design patterns.

IEnumerable interface

```
public interface IEnumerable {
  IEnumerator GetEnumerator( );
}
```

The C# foreach statement works on any collection that implements the IEnumerable interface. The IEnumerable interface has a single method that returns an IEnumerator object.

IEnumerator interface

```
public interface IEnumerator {
    bool MoveNext( );
    object Current {get;}
    void Reset( );
}
```

The IEnumerator interface provides a standard way to iterate over collections. Internally, an IEnumerator maintains the current position of an item in the collection. If the items are numbered 0 (inclusive) to n (exclusive), the current position starts off as -1, and finishes at n.

IEnumerator is typically implemented as a nested type and is initialized by passing the collection to the constructor of the IEnumerator:

```
using System;
using System.Collections;
public class MyCollection : IEnumerable {
    // Contents of this collection.
    private string[] items = {"hello", "world"};
    // Accessors for this collection.
    public string this[int index] {
        get { return items[index]; }
    }
    public int Count {
        get { return items.Length; }
    }
    // Implement IEnumerable.
    public virtual IEnumerator GetEnumerator ( ) {
        return new MyCollection.Enumerator(this);
    }
    // Define a custom enumerator.
    private class Enumerator : IEnumerator {
        private MyCollection collection;
        private int currentIndex = -1;
        internal Enumerator (MyCollection collection) {
            this.collection = collection;
        }
        public object Current {
            get {
                if (currentIndex==-1 || currentIndex == collection.Count)
                    throw new InvalidOperationException( );
                return collection [currentIndex];
            }
        }
        public bool MoveNext ( ) {
            if (currentIndex > collection.Count)
                throw new InvalidOperationException( );
            return ++currentIndex < collection.Count;
        }
        public void Reset ( ) {
```

```
            currentIndex = -1;
        }
    }
}
```

The collection can then be enumerated in either of these two ways:

```
MyCollection mcoll = new MyCollection();
// Using foreach: substitute your typename for string
foreach (string item in mcoll) {
  Console.WriteLine(item);
}
// Using IEnumerator: substitute your typename for string
IEnumerator ie = mcoll.GetEnumerator();
while (ie.MoveNext()) {
  string item = (string) ie.Current;
  Console.WriteLine(item);
}
```

ICollection interface

```
public interface ICollection : IEnumerable {
    void CopyTo(Array array, int index);
    int Count {get;}
    bool IsSynchronized {get;}
    object SyncRoot {get;}
}
```

ICollection is the interface implemented by all collections, including arrays, and provides the following methods:

CopyTo(Array *array*, int *index*)
> This method copies all the elements into the array starting at the specified index in the source collection.

Count
> This property returns the number of elements in the collection.

IsSynchronized( )
> This method allows you to determine whether or not a collection is thread-safe. The collections provided in the FCL are not themselves thread-safe, but each one includes a Synchronized method that returns a thread-safe wrapper of the collection.

SyncRoot( )
> This property returns an object (usually the collection itself) that can be locked to provide basic thread-safe support for the collection.

IComparer interface

IComparer is a standard interface that compares two objects for sorting in Arrays. You generally don't need to implement this interface, since a default

---

implementation that uses the IComparable interface is already provided by the Comparer type, which is used by the Array type.

```
public interface IComparer {
    int Compare(object x, object y);
}
```

IList interface

IList is an interface for array-indexable collections, such as ArrayList.

```
public interface IList : ICollection, IEnumerable {
    object this [int index] {get; set}
    bool IsFixedSize { get; }
    bool IsReadOnly { get; }
    int Add(object o);
    void Clear();
    bool Contains(object value);
    int IndexOf(object value);
    void Insert(int index, object value);
    void Remove(object value);
    void RemoveAt(int index);
}
```

IDictionary interface

IDictionary is an interface for key/value-based collections, such as Hashtable and SortedList.

```
public interface IDictionary : ICollection, IEnumerable {
    object this [object key] {get; set};
    bool IsFixedSize { get; }
    bool IsReadOnly { get; }
    ICollection Keys {get;}
    ICollection Values {get;}
    void Clear();
    bool Contains(object key);
    IDictionaryEnumerator GetEnumerator();
    void Remove(object key);
}
```

IDictionaryEnumerator interface

IDictionaryEnumerator is a standardized interface that enumerates over the contents of a dictionary.

```
public interface IDictionaryEnumerator : IEnumerator {
    DictionaryEntry Entry {get;}
    object Key {get;}
    object Value {get;}
}
```

IHashCodeProvider interface

IHashCodeProvider is a standard interface used by the Hashtable collection to hash its objects for storage.

```
public interface IHashCodeProvider {
    int GetHashCode(object o);
}
```

Regular Expressions

The FCL includes support for performing regular expression matching and replacement capabilities. The expressions are based on Perl5 *regexp*, including lazy quantifiers (e.g., ??, *?, +?, and {n,m}?), positive and negative lookahead, and conditional evaluation.

The types mentioned in this section all exist in the System.Text. RegularExpressions namespace.

Regex Class

The Regex class is the heart of the FCL regular expression support. Used both as an object instance and a static type, the Regex class represents an immutable, compiled instance of a regular expression that can be applied to a string via a matching process.

Internally, the regular expression is stored as either a sequence of internal regular expression bytecodes that are interpreted at match time or as compiled MSIL opcodes that are JIT-compiled by the CLR at runtime. This allows you to make a tradeoff between worsened regular expression startup time and memory utilization versus higher raw match performance at runtime.

For more information on the regular expression options, supported character escapes, substitution patterns, character sets, positioning assertions, quantifiers, grouping constructs, backreferences, and alternation, see Appendix B.

Match and MatchCollection Classes

The Match class represents the result of applying a regular expression to a string, looking for the first successful match. The MatchCollection class contains a collection of Match instances that represent the result of applying a regular expression to a string recursively until the first unsuccessful match occurs.

Group Class

The Group class represents the results from a single grouping expression. From this class, it is possible to drill down to the individual subexpression matches with the Captures property.

Capture and CaptureCollection Classes

The CaptureCollection class contains a collection of Capture instances, each representing the results of a single subexpression match.

Using Regular Expressions

Combining these classes, you can create the following example:

```
/*
 * Sample showing multiple groups
 * and groups with multiple captures
 */
using System;
using System.Text.RegularExpressions;
class Test {
  static void Main( ) {
    string text = "abracadabra1abracadabra2abracadabra3";
    string pat = @"
      (         # start the first group
        abra    # match the literal 'abra'
        (       # start the second (inner) group
        cad     # match the literal 'cad'
        )?      # end the second (optional) group
      )         # end the first group
      +         # match one or more occurences
    ";
    Console.WriteLine("Original text = [{0}]", text);
    // Create the Regex. IgnorePatternWhitespace permits
    // whitespace and comments.
    Regex r = new Regex(pat, RegexOptions.IgnorePatternWhitespace);
    int[] gnums = r.GetGroupNumbers( ); // get the list of group numbers
    Match m = r.Match(text); // get first match
    while (m.Success) {
      Console.WriteLine("Match found:");
      // start at group 1
      for (int i = 1; i < gnums.Length; i++) {
        Group g = m.Groups[gnums[i]]; // get the group for this match
        Console.WriteLine("\tGroup{0}=[{1}]", gnums[i], g);
        CaptureCollection cc = g.Captures; // get caps for this group
        for (int j = 0; j < cc.Count; j++) {
          Capture c = cc[j];
          Console.WriteLine("\t\tCapture{0}=[{1}] Index={2} Length={3}",
                            j, c, c.Index, c.Length);
```

```
            }
        }
        m = m.NextMatch(); // get next match
    } // end while
  }
}
```

The preceding example produces the following output:

```
Original text = [abracadabra1abracadabra2abracadabra3]
Match found:
        Group1=[abra]
                Capture0=[abracad] Index=0 Length=7
                Capture1=[abra] Index=7 Length=4
        Group2=[cad]
                Capture0=[cad] Index=4 Length=3
Match found:
        Group1=[abra]
                Capture0=[abracad] Index=12 Length=7
                Capture1=[abra] Index=19 Length=4
        Group2=[cad]
                Capture0=[cad] Index=16 Length=3
Match found:
        Group1=[abra]
                Capture0=[abracad] Index=24 Length=7
                Capture1=[abra] Index=31 Length=4
        Group2=[cad]
                Capture0=[cad] Index=28 Length=3
```

Input/Output

The FCL provides a streams-based I/O framework that can handle a wide range of stream and backing store types. This support for streams also infuses the rest of the FCL, with the pattern repeating in non-I/O areas such as cryptography, HTTP support, and more.

This section describes the core stream types and provides examples. The types mentioned in this section all exist in the System.IO namespace.

Streams and Backing Stores

A *stream* represents the flow of data coming in and out of a backing store. A *backing store* represents the endpoint of a stream. Although a backing store is often a file or network connection, in reality it can represent any medium capable of reading or writing raw data.

A simple example would be to use a stream to read and write to a file on disk. However, streams and backing stores are not limited to disk and network I/O. A more sophisticated example would be to use the cryptography support in the FCL to encrypt or decrypt a stream of bytes as they move around in memory.

Abstract Stream class

Stream is an abstract class that defines operations for reading and writing a stream of raw, typeless data as bytes. Once a stream has been opened, it stays open and can be read from or written to until the stream is flushed and closed. Flushing a stream updates the writes made to the stream; closing a stream first flushes the stream, then closes the stream.

Stream has the properties CanRead, CanWrite, Length, CanSeek, and Position. CanSeek is true if the stream supports random access and false if it only supports sequential access. If a stream supports random access, set the Position property to move to a linear position on that stream.

The Stream class provides synchronous and asynchronous read and write operations. By default, an asynchronous method calls the stream's corresponding synchronous method by wrapping the synchronous method in a delegate type and starting a new thread. Similarly, by default, a synchronous method calls the stream's corresponding asynchronous method and waits until the thread has completed its operation. Classes that derive from Stream must override either the synchronous or asynchronous methods but may override both sets of methods if the need arises.

Concrete Stream-derived classes

The FCL includes a number of different concrete implementations of the abstract base class Stream. Each implementation represents a different storage medium and allows a raw stream of bytes to be read from and written to the backing store.

Examples of this include the FileStream class (which reads and writes bytes to and from a file) and the System.Net.Sockets.NetworkStream class (which sends and receives bytes over the network).

In addition, a stream may act as the frontend to another stream, performing additional processing on the underlying stream as needed. Examples of this include stream encryption/decryption and stream buffering.

Here is an example that creates a text file on disk and uses the abstract Stream type to write data to it:

```
using System.IO;
class Test {
  static void Main( ) {
    Stream s = new FileStream("foo.txt", FileMode.Create);
    s.WriteByte(67);
```

```
        s.WriteByte(35);
        s.Close();
    }
}
```

Encapsulating raw streams

The Stream class defines operations for reading and writing raw, typeless data in the form of bytes. Typically, however, you need to work with a stream of characters, not a stream of bytes. To solve this problem, the FCL provides the abstract base classes TextReader and TextWriter, which define a contract to read and write a stream of characters, as well as a set of concrete implementations.

Abstract TextReader/TextWriter classes

TextReader and TextWriter are abstract base classes that define operations for reading and writing a stream of characters. The most fundamental operations of the TextReader and TextWriter classes are the methods that read and write a single character to or from a stream.

The TextReader class provides default implementations for methods that read in an array of characters or a string representing a line of characters. The TextWriter class provides default implementations for methods that write an array of characters, as well as methods that convert common types (optionally with formatting options) to a sequence of characters.

The FCL includes a number of different concrete implementations of the abstract base classes TextReader and TextWriter. Some of the most prominent include StreamReader and StreamWriter, and StringReader and StringWriter.

StreamReader and StreamWriter classes

StreamReader and StreamWriter are concrete classes that derive from TextReader and TextWriter, respectively, and operate on a Stream (passed as a constructor parameter).

These classes allow you to combine a Stream (which can have a backing store but only knows about raw data) with a TextReader/TextWriter (which knows about character data, but doesn't have a backing store).

In addition, StreamReader and StreamWriter can perform special translations between characters and raw bytes. Such translations include translating Unicode characters to ANSI characters to either big- or little-endian format.

Here is an example that uses a StreamWriter wrapped around a FileStream class to write to a file:

```
using System.Text;
using System.IO;
class Test {
  static void Main() {
    Stream fs = new FileStream ("foo.txt", FileMode.Create);
    StreamWriter sw = new StreamWriter(fs, Encoding.ASCII);
    sw.Write("Hello!");
    sw.Close();
  }
}
```

StringReader and StringWriter classes

StringReader and StringWriter are concrete classes that derive from
TextReader and TextWriter, respectively, and operate on a string (passed as a
constructor parameter).

The StringReader class can be thought of as the simplest possible read-only
backing store because it simply performs read operations on that string. The
StringWriter class can be thought of as the simplest possible write-only
backing store because it simply performs write operations on that
StringBuilder.

Here is an example that uses a StringWriter wrapped around an underlying
StringBuilder backing store to write to a string:

```
using System;
using System.IO;
using System.Text;
class Test {
  static void Main() {
    StringBuilder sb = new StringBuilder();
    StringWriter sw = new StringWriter(sb);
    WriteHello(sw);
    Console.WriteLine(sb);
  }
  static void WriteHello(TextWriter tw) {
    tw.Write("Hello, String I/O!");
  }
}
```

Directories and Files

The File and Directory classes encapsulate the operations typically associated with file I/O, such as copying, moving, deleting, renaming, and enu-
merating files and directories.

The actual manipulation of the contents of a file is done with a FileStream.
The File class has methods that return a FileStream, though you may
directly instantiate a FileStream.

In this example, you read in and print out the first line of a text file specified on the command line:

```
using System;
using System.IO;
class Test {
    static void Main(string[] args) {
        Stream s = File.OpenRead(args[0]);
        StreamReader sr = new StreamReader(s);
        Console.WriteLine(sr.ReadLine());
        sr.Close();
    }
}
```

Networking

The FCL includes a number of types that make accessing networked resources easy. Offering different levels of abstraction, these types allow an application to ignore much of the detail normally required to access networked resources, while retaining a high degree of control.

This section describes the core networking support in the FCL and provides numerous examples leveraging the predefined classes. The types mentioned in this section all exist in the System.Net and System.Net.Sockets namespaces.

Network Programming Models

High-level access is performed using a set of types that implement a generic request/response architecture that is extensible to support new protocols. The implementation of this architecture in the FCL also includes HTTP-specific extensions to make interacting with web servers easy.

Should the application require lower-level access to the network, types exist to support the Transmission Control Protocol (TCP) and User Datagram Protocol (UDP). Finally, in situations in which direct transport-level access is required, there are types that provide raw socket access.

Generic Request/Response Architecture

The request/response architecture is based on Uniform Resource Indicator (URI) and stream I/O, follows the factory design pattern, and makes good use of abstract types and interfaces.

A factory type (WebRequest) parses the URI and creates the appropriate protocol handler to fulfill the request.

Protocol handlers share a common abstract base type (WebRequest) that exposes properties that configure the request and methods used to retrieve the response.

Responses are also represented as types and share a common abstract base type (WebResponse) that exposes a Stream, providing simple streams-based I/O and easy integration into the rest of the FCL.

This example is a simple implementation of the popular Unix *snarf* utility. It demonstrates the use of the WebRequest and WebResponse classes to retrieve the contents of a URI and print them to the console:

```
// Snarf.cs
// Run Snarf.exe <http-uri> to retrieve a web page
using System;
using System.IO;
using System.Net;
using System.Text;
class Snarf {
  static void Main(string[] args) {

    // Retrieve the data at the URL with an WebRequest ABC
    WebRequest req = WebRequest.Create(args[0]);
    WebResponse resp = req.GetResponse( );

    // Read in the data, performing ASCII->Unicode encoding
    Stream s = resp.GetResponseStream( );
    StreamReader sr = new StreamReader(s, Encoding.ASCII);
    string doc = sr.ReadToEnd( );

    Console.WriteLine(doc); // Print result to console
  }
}
```

HTTP-Specific Support

The request/response architecture inherently supports protocol-specific extensions via the use of subtyping.

Since the WebRequest creates and returns the appropriate handler type based on the URI, accessing protocol-specific features is as easy as downcasting the returned WebRequest object to the appropriate protocol-specific handler and accessing the extended functionality.

The FCL includes specific support for the HTTP protocol, including the ability to easily access and control elements of an interactive web session, such as the HTTP headers, user-agent strings, proxy support, user credentials, authentication, keep-alives, pipelining, and more.

This example demonstrates the use of the HTTP-specific request/response classes to control the user-agent string for the request and retrieve the server type:

```
// ProbeSvr.cs
// Run ProbeSvr.exe <servername> to retrieve the server type
using System;
using System.Net;
class ProbeSvr {
  static void Main(string[] args) {

    // Get instance of WebRequest ABC, convert to HttpWebRequest
    WebRequest req = WebRequest.Create(args[0]);
    HttpWebRequest httpReq = (HttpWebRequest)req;

    // Access HTTP-specific features such as User-Agent
    httpReq.UserAgent = "CSPRProbe/1.0";

    // Retrieve response and print to console
    WebResponse resp = req.GetResponse();
    HttpWebResponse httpResp = (HttpWebResponse)resp;
    Console.WriteLine(httpResp.Server);
  }
}
```

Adding New Protocol Handlers

Adding handlers to support new protocols is trivial: simply implement a new set of derived types based on WebRequest and WebResponse, implement the IWebRequestCreate interface on your WebRequest-derived type, and register it as a new protocol handler with Web-Request.RegisterPrefix() at runtime. Once this is done, any code that uses the request/response architecture can access networked resources using the new URI format (and underlying protocol).

Using TCP, UDP, and Sockets

The System.Net.Sockets namespace includes types that provide protocol-level support for TCP and UDP. These types are built on the underlying Socket type, which is itself directly accessible for transport-level access to the network.

Two classes provide the TCP support: TcpListener and TcpClient. TcpListener listens for incoming connections, creating Socket instances that respond to the connection request. TcpClient connects to a remote host, hiding the details of the underlying socket in a Stream-derived type that allows stream I/O over the network.

A class called UdpClient provides the UDP support. UdpClient serves as both a client and a listener and includes multicast support, allowing individual datagrams to be sent and received as byte arrays.

Both the TCP and the UDP classes help access the underlying network socket (represented by the Socket class). The Socket class is a thin wrapper over the native Windows sockets functionality and is the lowest level of networking accessible to managed code.

The following example is a simple implementation of the Quote of the Day (QUOTD) protocol, as defined by the IETF in RFC 865. It demonstrates the use of a TCP listener to accept incoming requests and the use of the lower-level Socket type to fulfill the request:

```
// QOTDListener.cs
// Run QOTDListener.exe to service incoming QOTD requests
using System;
using System.Net;
using System.Net.Sockets;
using System.Text;
class QOTDListener {
  static string[] quotes = {
    @"Sufficiently advanced magic is indistinguishable from technology
        -- Terry Pratchett",
    @"Sufficiently advanced technology is indistinguishable from magic
        -- Arthur C. Clarke" };
  static void Main( ) {

    // Start a TCP listener on port 17
    TcpListener l = new TcpListener(17);
    l.Start( );
    Console.WriteLine("Waiting for clients to connect");
    Console.WriteLine("Press Ctrl+C to quit...");
    int numServed = 1;
    while (true) {

      // Block waiting for an incoming socket connect request
      Socket s = l.AcceptSocket( );

      // Encode alternating quotes as bytes for sending
      Char[] carr = quotes[numServed%2].ToCharArray( );
      Byte[] barr = Encoding.ASCII.GetBytes(carr);

      // Return data to client, then clean up socket and repeat
      s.Send(barr, barr.Length, 0);
      s.Shutdown(SocketShutdown.Both);
      s.Close( );
      Console.WriteLine("{0} quotes served...", numServed++);
    }
  }
}
```

To test this example, run the listener and try connecting to port 17 on *local-host* using a *telnet* client. (Under Windows, this can be done from the command line by entering telnet localhost 17).

Notice the use of Socket.Shutdown and Socket.Close at the end of the while loop. This is required to flush and close the socket immediately, rather than wait for the garbage collector to finalize and collect unreachable Socket objects later.

Using DNS

The networking types in the base class library also support normal and reverse Domain Name System (DNS) resolution. Here's an example using these types:

```
// DNSLookup.cs
// Run DNSLookup.exe <servername> to determine IP addresses
using System;
using System.Net;
class DNSLookup {
  static void Main(string[] args) {
    IPHostEntry he = Dns.GetHostByName(args[0]);
    IPAddress[] addrs = he.AddressList;
    foreach (IPAddress addr in addrs)
      Console.WriteLine(addr);
  }
}
```

Threading

A C# application runs in one or more *threads* that effectively execute in parallel within the same application. Here is a simple multithreaded application:

```
using System;
using System.Threading;
class ThreadTest {
  static void Main() {
    Thread t = new Thread(new ThreadStart(Go));
    t.Start();
    Go();
  }
  static void Go() {
    for (char c='a'; c<='z'; c++ )
      Console.Write(c);
  }
}
```

In this example, a new thread object is constructed by passing it a ThreadStart delegate that wraps the method that specifies where to start execution for that thread. You then start the thread and call Go, so two separate threads are running Go in parallel. However, there's a problem: both threads share a common resource—the console. If you run ThreadTest, you could get output like this:

```
abcdabcdefghijklmnopqrsefghijklmnopqrstuvwxyztuvwxyz
```

Thread Synchronization

Thread synchronization comprises techniques for ensuring that multiple threads coordinate their access to shared resources.

The lock statement

C# provides the lock statement to ensure that only one thread at a time can access a block of code. Consider the following example:

```
using System;
using System.Threading;
class LockTest {
  static void Main( ) {
    LockTest lt = new LockTest ( );
    Thread t = new Thread(new ThreadStart(lt.Go));
    t.Start( );
    lt.Go( );
  }
  void Go( ) {
    lock(this)
      for ( char c='a'; c<='z'; c++)
        Console.Write(c);
  }
}
```

Running LockTest produces the following output:

```
abcdefghijklmnopqrstuvwxyzabcdefghijklmnopqrstuvwxyz
```

The lock statement acquires a lock on any reference-type instance. If another thread has already acquired the lock, the thread doesn't continue until the other thread relinquishes its lock on that instance.

The lock statement is actually a syntactic shortcut for calling the Enter and Exit methods of the FCL Monitor class (see the later section "Monitor Class"):

```
System.Threading.Monitor.Enter(expression);
try {
  ...
}
finally {
  System.Threading.Monitor.Exit(expression);
}
```

Pulse and Wait operations

In combination with locks, the next most common threading operations are Pulse and Wait. These operations let threads communicate with each other via a monitor that maintains a list of threads waiting to grab an object's lock:

```
using System;
using System.Threading;
class MonitorTest {
  static void Main( ) {
    MonitorTest mt = new MonitorTest( );
    Thread t = new Thread(new ThreadStart(mt.Go));
    t.Start( );
    mt.Go( );
  }
  void Go( ) {
    for ( char c='a'; c<='z'; c++)
      lock(this) {
        Console.Write(c);
        Monitor.Pulse(this);
        Monitor.Wait(this);
      }
  }
}
```

Running MonitorTest produces the following result:

```
aabbccddeeffgghhiijjkkllmmnnooppqqrrssttuuvvwwxxyyzz
```

The Pulse method tells the monitor to wake up the next thread that is waiting to get a lock on that object as soon as the current thread has released it. The current thread typically releases the monitor in one of two ways. First, execution may leave the scope of the lock statement block. The second way is to call the Wait method, which temporarily releases the lock on an object and makes the thread fall asleep until another thread wakes it up by pulsing the object.

Deadlocks

The MonitorTest example actually contains a bug. When you run the program, it prints the correct output, but then the console window locks up. This occurs because the last thread printing z goes to sleep but never gets pulsed. You can solve the problem by replacing the Go method with this new implementation:

```
void Go( ) {
  for ( char c='a'; c<='z'; c++)
    lock(this) {
      Console.Write(c);
      Monitor.Pulse(this);
```

```
      if (c<'z')
        Monitor.Wait(this);
    }
  }
```

In general, the danger of using locks is that two threads may both end up being blocked waiting for a resource held by the other thread. This situation is known as a deadlock. Most common deadlock situations can be avoided by ensuring that you always acquire resources in the same order.

Atomic operations

Atomic operations are operations the system promises will not be interrupted. In the previous examples, the Go method isn't atomic because it can be interrupted while it is running so another thread can run. However, updating a variable is atomic because the operation is guaranteed to complete without control being passed to another thread. The Interlocked class provides additional atomic operations, which allows basic operations to be performed without requiring a lock. This can be useful, since acquiring a lock is many times slower than a simple atomic operation.

Common Thread Types

Much of the functionality of threads is provided through the classes in the System.Threading namespace. The most basic thread class to understand is the Monitor class, which is explained in the following section.

Monitor Class

The System.Threading.Monitor class provides an implementation of Hoare's Monitor that allows you to use any reference-type instance as a monitor.

Enter and Exit methods

The Enter and Exit methods, respectively, obtain and release a lock on an object. If the object is already held by another thread, Enter waits until the lock is released or the thread is interrupted by a Thread-InterruptedException. Every call to Enter for a given object on a thread should be matched with a call to Exit for the same object on the same thread.

TryEnter methods

The TryEnter methods are similar to the Enter method but don't require a lock on the object to proceed. These methods return true if the lock is

---

obtained and false if it isn't, optionally passing in a timeout parameter that specifies the maximum time to wait for the other threads to relinquish the lock.

Wait methods

The thread holding a lock on an object may call one of the Wait methods to temporarily release the lock and block itself while it waits for another thread to notify it by executing a pulse on the monitor. This approach can tell a worker thread that there is work to perform on that object. The overloaded versions of Wait allow you to specify a timeout that reactivates the thread if a pulse hasn't arrived within the specified duration. When the thread wakes up, it reacquires the monitor for the object (potentially blocking until the monitor becomes available). Wait returns true if the thread is reactivated by another thread pulsing the monitor and returns false if the Wait call times out without receiving a pulse.

Pulse and PulseAll methods

A thread holding a lock on an object may call Pulse on that object to wake up a blocked thread as soon as the thread calling Pulse has released its lock on the monitor. If multiple threads are waiting on the same monitor, Pulse activates only the first in the queue (successive calls to Pulse wake up other waiting threads, one per call). The PulseAll method successively wakes up all the threads.

Assemblies

An *assembly* is a logical package (similar to a DLL in Win32) that consists of a manifest, a set of one or more modules, and an optional set of resources. This package forms the basic unit of deployment and versioning, and creates a boundary for type resolution and security permissioning.

Elements of an Assembly

Every .NET application consists of at least one assembly, which is in turn built from a number of basic elements.

The *manifest* contains a set of metadata that describes everything the runtime needs to know about the assembly. This information includes:

- The textual name of the assembly
- The version number of the assembly
- An optional shared name and signed assembly hash

- The list of files in the assembly with file hashes
- The list of referenced assemblies, including versioning information and an optional public key
- The list of types included in the assembly, with a mapping to the module containing the type
- The set of minimum and optional security permissions requested by the assembly
- The set of security permissions explicitly refused by the assembly
- Culture, processor, and OS information
- A set of custom attributes to capture details such as product name, owner information, etc.

Modules contain types described using metadata and implemented using MSIL.

Resources contain nonexecutable data that is logically included with the assembly. Examples of this include bitmaps, localizable text, persisted objects, etc.

Packaging

The simplest assembly contains a manifest and a single module containing the application's types, packaged as an EXE with a Main entry point. More complex assemblies can include multiple modules (Portable Executable (PE) files), separate resource files, a manifest, etc.

The manifest is generally included in one of the existing PE files in the assembly, although the manifest can also be a standalone PE file.

Modules are PE files, typically DLLs or EXEs. Only one module in an assembly can contain an entry point (either Main, WinMain, or DllMain).

An assembly may also contain multiple modules. This technique can reduce the working set of the application, because the CLR loads only the required modules. In addition, each module can be written in a different language, allowing a mixture of C#, VB.NET, and raw MSIL. Although not common, a single module can also be included in several different assemblies.

Finally, an assembly may contain a set of resources, which can be kept either in standalone files or included in one of the PE files in the assembly.

Deployment

An assembly is the smallest .NET unit of deployment. Due to the self-describing nature of a manifest, deployment can be as simple as copying the assembly (and in the case of a multifile assembly, all the associated files) into a directory.

This is a vast improvement over traditional COM development in which components, their supporting DLLs, and their configuration information are spread out over multiple directories and the Windows registry.

Generally, assemblies are deployed into the application directory and are not shared. These are called *private assemblies*. However, assemblies can also be shared between applications; these are called *shared assemblies*. To share an assembly you need to give it a *shared name* (also known as a "strong" name) and deploy it in the global assembly cache.

The shared name consists of a name, a public key, and a digital signature. The shared name is included in the assembly manifest and forms the unique identifier for the assembly.

The global assembly cache is a machine-wide storage area that contains assemblies intended for use by multiple applications.

For more information on working with shared assemblies and the global assembly cache, see "Sharing Assemblies" in Appendix E.

Versioning

The manifest of an application contains a version number for the assembly and a list of all the referenced assemblies with associated version information. Assembly version numbers are divided into four parts and look like this:

```
<major>.<minor>.<build>.<revision>
```

This information is used to mitigate versioning problems as assemblies evolve over time.

At runtime, the CLR uses the version information specified in the manifest and a set of versioning policies defined for the machine to determine which versions of each dependent, shared assembly to load.

The default versioning policy for shared assemblies restricts you to the version that your application was built against. By changing a configuration file, the application or an administrator can override this behavior.

Private assemblies have no versioning policy, and the CLR simply loads the newest assemblies found in the application directory.

Type Resolution

The unique identifier for a type (known as a `TypeRef`) consists of a reference to the assembly it was defined in and the fully qualified type name (including any namespaces). For example, this local variable declaration:

```
System.Xml.XmlReader xr;
```

is represented in MSIL assembly language as follows:

```
.assembly extern System.Xml { .ver 1:0:3300:0 ... }
.locals init (class [System.Xml]System.Xml.XmlReader V_0)
```

In this example, the `System.Xml.XmlReader` type is scoped to the `System.Xml` shared assembly, which is identified using a shared name and associated version number.

When your application starts, the CLR attempts to resolve all static Type-Refs by locating the correct versions of each dependent assembly (as determined by the versioning policy) and verifying that the types actually exist (ignoring any access modifiers).

When your application attempts to use the type, the CLR verifies that you have the correct level of access and throws runtime exceptions if there is a versioning incompatibility.

Security Permissions

The assembly forms a boundary for security permissioning.

The assembly manifest contains hashes for any referenced assemblies (determined at compile time), a list of the minimum set of security permissions the assembly *requires* in order to function, a list of the optional permissions that it *requests*, and a list of the permissions that it explicitly *refuses* (i.e., never wants to receive).

To illustrate how these permissions might be used, imagine an email client similar to Microsoft Outlook, developed using the .NET Framework. It probably requires the ability to communicate over the network on ports 110 (POP3), 25 (SMTP), and 143 (IMAP4). It might request the ability to run Java Script functions in a sandbox to allow for full interactivity when presenting HTML emails. Finally, it probably refuses ever being granted the ability to write to disk or read the local address book, thus avoiding scripting attacks such as the *ILoveYou* virus.

Essentially, the assembly declares its security needs and assumptions, but leaves the final decision on permissioning up to the CLR, which enforces local security policy.

At runtime the CLR uses the hashes to determine if a dependent assembly has been tampered with and combines the assembly permission information with local security policy to determine whether to load the assembly and which permissions to grant it.

This mechanism provides fine-grained control over security and is a major advantage of the .NET Framework over traditional Windows applications.

Reflection

Many of the services available in .NET and exposed via C# (such as late binding, serialization, remoting, attributes, etc.) depend on the presence of metadata. Your own programs can also take advantage of this metadata and even extend it with new information.

Manipulating existing types via their metadata is termed *reflection* and is done using a rich set of types in the System.Reflection namespace. Creating new types (and associated metadata) is termed Reflection.Emit and is done via the types in the System.Reflection.Emit namespace. You can extend the metadata for existing types with custom attributes. For more information, see "Custom Attributes" later in this chapter.

Type Hierarchy

Reflection involves traversing and manipulating an object model that represents an application, including all its compile-time and runtime elements. Consequently, it is important to understand the various logical units of a .NET application and their roles and relationships.

The fundamental units of an application are its types, which contain members and nested types. In addition to types, an application contains one or more modules and one or more assemblies. All these elements are static and are described in metadata produced by the compiler at compile time. The one exception to this rule is elements (such as types, modules, assemblies, etc.) that are created on the fly via Reflection.Emit, which is described in the later section "Creating New Types at Runtime."

At runtime, these elements are all contained within an AppDomain. An AppDomain isn't described with metadata, yet it plays an important role in reflection because it forms the root of the type hierarchy of a .NET application at runtime.

In any given application, the relationship between these units is hierarchical, as depicted by the following diagram:

```
AppDomain (runtime root of hierarchy)
  Assemblies
```

```
Modules
  Types
    Members
    Nested types
```

Each of these elements is discussed in the following sections.

Types, members, and nested types

The most basic element that reflection deals with is the type. This class represents the metadata for each type declaration in an application (both predefined and user-defined types).

Types contain members, which include constructors, fields, properties, events, and methods. In addition, types may contain nested types, which exist within the scope of an outer type and are typically used as helper classes. Types are grouped into modules, which are, in turn, contained within assemblies.

Assemblies and modules

Assemblies are the logical equivalent of DLLs in Win32 and the basic units of deployment, versioning, and reuse for types. In addition, assemblies create a security, visibility, and scope resolution boundary for types (see the earlier section "Assemblies").

A module is a physical file such as a DLL, an EXE, or a resource (such as GIFs or JPGs). While it isn't common practice, an assembly can be composed of multiple modules, allowing you to control application working set size, use multiple languages within one assembly, and share a module across multiple assemblies.

AppDomains

From the perspective of reflection, an AppDomain is the root of the type hierarchy and serves as the container for assemblies and types when they are loaded into memory at runtime. A helpful way to think about an AppDomain is to view it as the logical equivalent of a process in a Win32 application.

AppDomains provide isolation, creating a hard boundary for managed code just like the process boundary under Win32. Similar to processes, AppDomains can be started and stopped independently, and application faults take down only the AppDomain the fault occurs in, not the process hosting the AppDomain.

Retrieving the Type for an Instance

At the heart of reflection is System.Type, which is an abstract base class that provides access to the metadata of a type.

You can access the Type class for any instance using GetType, which is a non-virtual method of System.Object. When you call GetType, the method returns a concrete subtype of System.Type, which can reflect over and manipulate the type.

Retrieving a Type Directly

You can also retrieve a Type class by name (without needing an instance) using the static method GetType on the Type class, as follows:

```
Type t = Type.GetType("System.Int32");
```

Finally, C# provides the typeof operator, which returns the Type class for any type known at compile time:

```
Type t = typeof(System.Int32);
```

The main difference between these two approaches is that Type.GetType is evaluated at runtime and is more dynamic, binding by name, while the typeof operator is evaluated at compile time, uses a type token, and is slightly faster to call.

Reflecting Over a Type Hierarchy

Once you have retrieved a Type instance you can navigate the application hierarchy described earlier, accessing the metadata via types that represent members, modules, assemblies, namespaces, AppDomains, and nested types. You can also inspect the metadata and any custom attributes, create new instances of the types, and invoke members.

Here is an example that uses reflection to display the members in three different types:

```
using System;
using System.Reflection;
class Test {
  static void Main( ) {
    object o = new Object( );
    DumpTypeInfo(o.GetType( ));
    DumpTypeInfo(typeof(int));
    DumpTypeInfo(Type.GetType("System.String"));
  }
  static void DumpTypeInfo(Type t) {
    Console.WriteLine("Type: {0}", t);
```

```
// Retrieve the list of members in the type
MemberInfo[] miarr = t.GetMembers();

// Print out details on each of them
foreach (MemberInfo mi in miarr)
  Console.WriteLine("  {0}={1}", mi.MemberType, mi);
  }
}
```

Late Binding to Types

Reflection can also perform *late binding*, in which the application dynamically loads, instantiates, and uses a type at runtime. This provides greater flexibility at the expense of invocation overhead.

In this section, we create an example that uses very late binding, dynamically discovers new types at runtime, and uses them.

In the example one or more assemblies are loaded by name (as specified on the command line) and iterated through the types in the assembly, looking for subtypes of the Greeting abstract base class. When one is found, the type is instantiated and its SayHello method invoked, which displays an appropriate greeting.

To perform the runtime discovery of types, we use an abstract base class that's compiled into an assembly as follows (see the source comment for filename and compilation information):

```
// Greeting.cs - compile with /t:library
public abstract class Greeting {
  public abstract void SayHello();
}
```

Compiling this code produces a file named *Greeting.dll*, which the other parts of the sample can use.

We now create a new assembly containing two concrete subtypes of the abstract type Greeting, as follows (see the source comment for filename and compilation information):

```
// English.cs - compile with /t:library /r:Greeting.dll
using System;
public class AmericanGreeting : Greeting {
  private string msg = "Hey, dude. Wassup!";
  public override void SayHello() {
    Console.WriteLine(msg);
  }
}
public class BritishGreeting : Greeting {
  private string msg = "Good morning, old chap!";
  public override void SayHello() {
```

```
      Console.WriteLine(msg);
  }
}
```

Compiling the source file *English.cs* produces a file named *English.dll,* which the main program can now dynamically reflect over and use.

Now we create the main sample, as follows (see the source comment for file-name and compilation information):

```
// SayHello.cs - compile with /r:Greeting.dll
// Run with SayHello.exe <dllname1> <dllname2> ... <dllnameN>
using System;
using System.Reflection;
class Test {
  static void Main (string[] args) {

    // Iterate over the cmd-line options,
    // trying to load each assembly
    foreach (string s in args) {
      Assembly a = Assembly.LoadFrom(s);

      // Pick through all the public type, looking for
      // subtypes of the abstract base class Greeting
      foreach (Type t in a.GetTypes())
        if (t.IsSubclassOf(typeof(Greeting))) {

          // Having found an appropriate subtype, create it
          object o = Activator.CreateInstance(t);

          // Retrieve the SayHello MethodInfo and invoke it
          MethodInfo mi = t.GetMethod("SayHello");
          mi.Invoke(o, null);
        }
    }
  }
}
```

Running the sample now with *SayHello English.dll* produces the following output:

```
Hey, dude. Wassup!
Good morning, old chap!
```

The interesting aspect of the preceding sample is that it's completely late-bound; i.e., long after the *SayHello* program is shipped you can create a new type and have *SayHello* automatically take advantage of it by simply specifying it on the command line. This is one of the key benefits of late binding via reflection.

Activation

In the previous examples, we loaded an assembly by hand and used the System.Activator class to create a new instance based on a type. There are many overrides of the CreateInstance method that provide a wide range of creation options, including the ability to short-circuit the process and create a type directly:

```
object o = Activator.CreateInstance("Assem1.dll",
                                    "Friendly.Greeting");
```

Other capabilities of the Activator type include creating types on remote machines, creating types in specific AppDomains (sandboxes), and creating types by invoking a specific constructor (rather than using the default constructor as these examples show).

Advanced Uses of Reflection

The preceding example demonstrates the use of reflection, but doesn't perform any tasks you can't accomplish using normal C# language constructs. However, reflection can also manipulate types in ways not supported directly in C#, as is demonstrated in this section.

While the CLR enforces access controls on type members (specified using access modifiers such as private and protected), these restrictions don't apply to reflection. Assuming you have the correct set of permissions, you can use reflection to access and manipulate private data and function members, as this example using the Greeting subtypes from the previous section shows (see the source comment for filename and compilation information):

```
// InControl.cs - compile with /r:Greeting.dll,English.dll
using System;
using System.Reflection;
class TestReflection {
  // Note: This method requires the ReflectionPermission perm.
  static void ModifyPrivateData(object o, string msg) {

    // Get a FieldInfo type for the private data member
    Type t = o.GetType();
    FieldInfo fi = t.GetField("msg", BindingFlags.NonPublic|
                                     BindingFlags.Instance);

    // Use the FieldInfo to adjust the data member value
    fi.SetValue(o, msg);
  }
  static void Main() {
    // Create instances of both types
    BritishGreeting bg = new BritishGreeting();
    AmericanGreeting ag = new AmericanGreeting();
```

```
// Adjust the private data via reflection
ModifyPrivateData(ag, "Things are not the way they seem");
ModifyPrivateData(bg, "The runtime is in total control!");

// Display the modified greeting strings
ag.SayHello( ); // "Things are not the way they seem"
bg.SayHello( ); // "The runtime is in total control!"
  }
}
```

When run, this sample generates the following output:

```
Things are not the way they seem
The runtime is in total control!
```

This demonstrates that the private msg data members in both types are modified via reflection, although there are no public members defined on the types that allow that operation. Note that while this technique can bypass access controls, it still doesn't violate type safety.

Although this is a somewhat contrived example, the capability can be useful when building utilities such as class browsers and test suite automation tools that need to inspect and interact with a type at a deeper level than its public interface.

Creating New Types at Runtime

The System.Reflection.Emit namespace contains classes that can create entirely new types at runtime. These classes can define a dynamic assembly in memory; define a dynamic module in the assembly; define a new type in the module, including all its members; and emit the MSIL opcodes needed to implement the application logic in the members.

Here is an example that creates and uses a new type called HelloWorld with a member called SayHello:

```
using System;
using System.Reflection;
using System.Reflection.Emit;
public class Test {
  static void Main( )  {
    // Create a dynamic assembly in the current AppDomain
    AppDomain ad = AppDomain.CurrentDomain;
    AssemblyName an = new AssemblyName( );
    an.Name = "DynAssembly";
    AssemblyBuilder ab =
      ad.DefineDynamicAssembly(an, AssemblyBuilderAccess.Run);

    // Create a module in the assembly and a type in the module
    ModuleBuilder modb = ab.DefineDynamicModule("DynModule");
    TypeBuilder tb = modb.DefineType("AgentSmith",
                                    TypeAttributes.Public);
```

```
      // Add a SayHello member to the type
      MethodBuilder mb = tb.DefineMethod("SayHello",
                                  MethodAttributes.Public,
                                  null, null);

      // Generate the MSIL for the SayHello Member
      ILGenerator ilg = mb.GetILGenerator( );
      ilg.EmitWriteLine("Never send a human to do a machine's job.");
      ilg.Emit(OpCodes.Ret);

      // Finalize the type so we can create it
      Type t = tb.CreateType( );

      // Create an instance of the new type
      object o = Activator.CreateInstance(t);

      // Prints "Never send a human to do a machine's job."
      t.GetMethod("SayHello").Invoke(o, null);
   }
}
```

A common example using Reflection.Emit is the regular expression support in the FCL, which can emit new types that are tuned to search for specific regular expressions, eliminating the overhead of interpreting the regular expression at runtime.

Other uses of Reflection.Emit in the FCL include dynamically generating transparent proxies for remoting and generating types that perform specific XSLT transforms with the minimum runtime overhead.

Custom Attributes

Types, members, modules, and assemblies all have associated metadata that is used by all the major CLR services, is considered an indivisible part of an application, and can be accessed via reflection (see the earlier section "Reflection").

A key characteristic of metadata is that it can be extended. You extend the metadata with *custom attributes*, which allow you to "decorate" a code element with additional information stored in the metadata associated with the element.

This additional information can then be retrieved at runtime and used to build services that work *declaratively*, which is the way that the CLR implements core features such as serialization and interception.

Language Support for Custom Attributes

Decorating an element with a custom attribute is known as *specifying* the custom attribute and is done by writing the name of the attribute enclosed in brackets ([ ]) immediately before the element declaration as follows:

```
[Serializable] public class Foo {...}
```

In this example, the Foo class is specified as serializable. This information is saved in the metadata for Foo and affects the way the CLR treats an instance of this class.

A useful way to think about custom attributes is that they expand the built-in set of declarative constructs such as public, private, and sealed in the C# language.

Compiler Support for Custom Attributes

In reality, custom attributes are simply types derived from System.Attribute with language constructs for specifying them on an element (see the section "Attributes" in Chapter 2).

These language constructs are recognized by the compiler, which emits a small chunk of data into the metadata. This custom data includes a serialized call to the constructor of the custom attribute type (containing the values for the positional parameters) and a collection of property set operations (containing the values for the named parameters).

The compiler also recognizes a small number of *pseudo-custom attributes*. These are special attributes that have direct representation in metadata and are stored natively (i.e., not as chunks of custom data). This is primarily a runtime performance optimization, although it has some implications for retrieving attributes via reflection, as discussed later.

To understand this, consider the following class with two specified attributes:

```
[Serializable, Obsolete]
class Foo {...}
```

When compiled, the metadata for the Foo class looks like this in MSIL:

```
.class private auto ansi serializable beforefieldinit Foo
       extends [mscorlib]System.Object
{
  .custom instance void
  [mscorlib]System.ObsoleteAttribute::.ctor( ) = ( 01 00 00 00 )
  ...
}
```

Compare the different treatment by the compiler of the Obsolete attribute, which is a custom attribute and represented by a .custom directive containing the serialized attribute parameters, to the treatment of the Serializable attribute, which is a pseudo-custom attribute represented directly in the metadata with the serializable token.

Runtime Support for Custom Attributes

At runtime the core CLR services such as serialization and remoting inspect the custom and pseudo-custom attributes to determine how to handle an instance of a type.

In the case of custom attributes, this is done by creating an instance of the attribute (invoking the relevant constructor call and property-set operations), and then performing whatever steps are needed to determine how to handle an instance of the type.

In the case of pseudo-custom attributes, this is done by simply inspecting the metadata directly and determining how to handle an instance of the type. Consequently, handling pseudo-custom attributes is more efficient than handling custom attributes.

Note that none of these steps is initiated until a service or user program actually tries to access the attributes, so there is little runtime overhead unless it is required.

Predefined Attributes

The .NET Framework makes extensive use of attributes for purposes ranging from simple documentation to advanced support for threading, remoting, serialization, and COM interop. These attributes are all defined in the FCL and can be used, extended, and retrieved by your own code.

However, certain attributes are treated specially by the compiler and the runtime. Three attributes considered general enough to be defined in the C# specification are AttributeUsage, Conditional, and Obsolete. Other attributes such as CLSCompliant, Serializable, and NonSerialized are also treated specially.

AttributeUsage attribute

Syntax:

```
[AttributeUsage(target-enum
    [, AllowMultiple=[true|false]]?
```

Syntax:

```
 [, Inherited=[true|false]]?
] (for classes)
```

The AttributeUsage attribute is applied to a new attribute class declaration. It controls how the new attribute should be treated by the compiler, specifically, what set of targets (classes, interfaces, properties, methods, parameters, etc.) the new attribute can be specified on, whether multiple instances of this attribute may be applied to the same target, and whether this attribute propagates to subtypes of the target.

target-enum is a bitwise mask of values from the System.AttributeTargets enum, which looks like this:

```
namespace System {
  [Flags]
  public enum AttributeTargets {
    Assembly     = 0x0001,
    Module       = 0x0002,
    Class        = 0x0004,
    Struct       = 0x0008,
    Enum         = 0x0010,
    Constructor  = 0x0020,
    Method       = 0x0040,
    Property     = 0x0080,
    Field        = 0x0100,
    Event        = 0x0200,
    Interface    = 0x0400,
    Parameter    = 0x0800,
    Delegate     = 0x1000,
    ReturnValue  = 0x2000,
    All          = 0x3fff,
  }
}
```

Conditional attribute

Syntax:

[Conditional(*symbol*)] *(for methods)*

The Conditional attribute can be applied to any method with a void return type. The presence of this attribute tells the compiler to conditionally omit calls to the method unless *symbol* is defined in the calling code. This is similar to wrapping every call to the method with #if and #endif preprocessor directives, but Conditional has the advantage of needing to be specified only in one place. Conditional can be found in the System.Diagnostics namespace.

Obsolete attribute

Syntax:

[Obsolete(*message*[, true | false]] *(for all attribute targets)*

Applied to any valid attribute target, the Obsolete attribute indicates that the target is obsolete. Obsolete can include a message that explains which alternative types or members to use and a flag that tells the compiler to treat the use of this type or member as either a warning or an error.

For example, referencing type Bar in the following example causes the compiler to display an error message and halts compilation:

```
[Obsolete("Don't try this at home", true)]
class Bar { ... }
```

CLSCompliant attribute

Syntax:

[CLSCompliant(true|false)] *(for all attribute targets)*

Applied to an assembly, the CLSCompliant attribute tells the compiler whether to validate CLS compliance for all the exported types in the assembly. Applied to any other attribute target, this attribute allows the target to declare if it should be considered CLS-compliant. In order to mark a target as CLS-compliant, the entire assembly needs to be considered as such.

In the following example, the CLSCompliant attribute is used to specify an assembly as CLS-compliant and a class within it as not CLS-compliant:

```
[assembly:CLSCompliant(true)]

[CLSCompliant(false)]
public class Bar {
  public ushort Answer { get {return 42;} }
}
```

Serializable attribute

Syntax:

[Serializable] *(for classes, structs, enums, delegates)*

Applied to a class, struct, enum, or delegate, the Serializable attribute marks it as being serializable. This attribute is a pseudo-custom attribute and is represented specially in the metadata.

NonSerialized attribute

Syntax:

[NonSerialized] *(for fields)*

Applied to a field, the NonSerialized attribute prevents it from being serialized along with its containing class or struct. This attribute is a pseudo-custom attribute and is represented specially in the metadata.

Defining a New Custom Attribute

In addition to using the predefined attributes supplied by the .NET Framework, you can also create your own.

To create a custom attribute:

1. Derive a class from System.Attribute or from a descendent of System. Attribute. By convention the class name should end with the word "Attribute," although this isn't required.

2. Provide the class with a public constructor. The parameters to the constructor define the positional parameters of the attribute and are mandatory when specifying the attribute on an element.

3. Declare public-instance fields, public-instance read/write properties, or public-instance write-only properties to specify the named parameters of the attribute. Unlike positional parameters, these are optional when specifying the attribute on an element.

   The types that can be used for attribute constructor parameters and properties are bool, byte, char, double, float, int, long, short, string, object, the Type type, enum, or a one-dimensional array of the aforementioned types.

4. Finally, define what the attribute may be specified on using the AttributeUsage attribute, as described in the preceding section.

Consider the following example of a custom attribute, CrossRef-Attribute, which removes the limitation that the CLR metadata contain information about statically linked types but not dynamically linked ones:

```
// XRef.cs - cross-reference custom attribute
// Compile with: csc /t:library XRef.cs
using System;
[AttributeUsage(AttributeTargets.All, AllowMultiple=true)]
public class CrossRefAttribute : Attribute {
  Type    xref;
  string desc = "";
  public string Description { set { desc=value; } }
  public CrossRefAttribute(Type xref) { this.xref=xref; }
  public override string ToString( ) {
    string tmp = (desc.Length>0) ? " ("+desc+")" : "";
    return "CrossRef to "+xref.ToString( )+tmp;
  }
}
```

From the attribute user's perspective, this attribute can be applied to any target multiple times (note the use of the `AttributeUsage` attribute to control this). `CrossRefAttribute` takes one mandatory positional parameter (namely the type to cross-reference) and one optional named parameter (the description), and is used as follows:

```
[CrossRef(typeof(Bar), Description="Foos often hang around Bars")]
class Foo {...}
```

Essentially, this attribute embeds cross-references to dynamically linked types (with optional descriptions) in the metadata. This information can then be retrieved at runtime by a class browser to present a more complete view of a type's dependencies.

Retrieving a Custom Attribute at Runtime

Retrieving attributes at runtime is done using reflection via one of `System.Attribute`'s `GetCustomAttribute` or `GetCustomAttributes` overloads. This is one of the few circumstances in which the difference between custom attributes and pseudo-custom attributes becomes apparent, since pseudo-custom attributes can't be retrieved with `GetCustomAttribute`.

Here is an example that uses reflection to determine which attributes are on a specific type:

```
using System;
[Serializable, Obsolete]
class Test {
  static void Main( ) {
    Type t = typeof(Test);
    object[] caarr = Attribute.GetCustomAttributes(t);
    Console.WriteLine("{0} has {1} custom attribute(s)",
                      t, caarr.Length);
    foreach (object ca in caarr)
      Console.WriteLine(ca);
  }
}
```

Although the `Test` class of the preceding example has two attributes specified, the sample produces the following output:

```
Test has 1 custom attribute(s)
System.ObsoleteAttribute
```

This demonstrates how the `Serializable` attribute (a pseudo-custom attribute) isn't accessible via reflection, while the `Obsolete` attribute (a custom attribute) still is.

Automatic Memory Management

Almost all modern programming languages allocate memory in two places: on the stack and on the heap.

Memory allocated on the stack stores local variables, parameters, and return values, and is generally managed automatically by the operating system.

Memory allocated on the heap, however, is treated differently by different languages. In C and C++, memory allocated on the heap is managed manually. In C# and Java, however, memory allocated on the heap is managed automatically.

While manual memory management has the advantage of being simple for runtimes to implement, it has drawbacks that tend not to exist in systems that offer automatic memory management. For example, a large percentage of bugs in C and C++ programs stem from using an object after it has been deleted (dangling pointers) or from forgetting to delete an object when it is no longer needed (memory leaks).

The process of automatically managing memory is known as *garbage collection*. While generally more complex for runtimes to implement than traditional manual memory management, garbage collection greatly simplifies development and eliminates many common errors related to manual memory management.

For example, it is almost impossible to generate a traditional memory leak in C#, and common bugs such as circular references in traditional COM development simply go away.

The Garbage Collector

C# depends on the CLR for many of its runtime services, and garbage collection is no exception.

The CLR includes a high-performing generational mark-and-compact garbage collector (GC) that performs automatic memory management for type instances stored on the managed heap.

The GC is considered to be a *tracing* garbage collector in that it doesn't interfere with every access to an object, but rather wakes up intermittently and traces the graph of objects stored on the managed heap to determine which objects can be considered garbage and therefore collected.

The GC generally initiates a garbage collection when a memory allocation occurs, and memory is too low to fulfill the request. This process can also be initiated manually using the System.GC type. Initiating a garbage collection freezes all threads in the process to allow the GC time to examine the managed heap.

The GC begins with the set of object references considered *roots* and walks the object graph, marking all the objects it touches as reachable. Once this process is complete, all objects that have not been marked are considered garbage.

Objects that are considered garbage and don't have finalizers are immediately discarded, and the memory is reclaimed. Objects that are considered garbage and do have finalizers are flagged for additional asynchronous processing on a separate thread to invoke their Finalize methods before they can be considered garbage and reclaimed at the next collection.

Objects considered still live are then shifted down to the bottom of the heap (*compacted*), hopefully freeing space to allow the memory allocation to succeed.

At this point the memory allocation is attempted again, the threads in the process are unfrozen, and either normal processing continues or an OutOfMemoryException is thrown.

Optimization Techniques

Although this may sound like an inefficient process compared to simply managing memory manually, the GC incorporates various optimization techniques to reduce the time an application is frozen waiting for the GC to complete (known as *pause time*).

The most important of these optimizations is what makes the GC generational. This techniques takes advantage of the fact that while many objects tend to be allocated and discarded rapidly, certain objects are long-lived and thus don't need to be traced during every collection.

Basically, the GC divides the managed heap into three *generations*. Objects that have just been allocated are considered to be in Gen0, objects that have survived one collection cycle are considered to be in Gen1, and all other objects are considered to be in Gen2.

When it performs a collection, the GC initially collects only Gen0 objects. If not enough memory is reclaimed to fulfill the request, both Gen0 and Gen1 objects are collected, and if that fails as well, a full collection of Gen0, Gen1, and Gen2 objects is attempted.

Many other optimizations are also used to enhance the performance of automatic memory management, and generally, a GC-based application can be expected to approach the performance of an application that uses manual memory management.

Finalizers

When implementing your own types, you can choose to give them *finalizers* (via C# destructors), which are methods called asynchronously by the GC once an object is determined to be garbage.

Although this is required in certain cases, generally, there are many good technical reasons to avoid the use of finalizers.

As described in the previous section, objects with finalizers incur significant overhead when they are collected, requiring asynchronous invocation of their `Finalize` methods and taking two full GC cycles for their memory to be reclaimed.

Other reasons not to use finalizers include:

- Objects with finalizers take longer to allocate on the managed heap than objects without finalizers.
- Objects with finalizers that refer to other objects (even those without finalizers) can prolong the life of the referred objects unnecessarily.
- It's impossible to predict in what order the finalizers for a set of objects will be called.
- You have limited control over when (or even if!) the finalizer for an object will be called.

In summary, finalizers are somewhat like lawyers: while there are cases when you really need them, generally, you don't want to use them unless absolutely necessary, and if you do use them, you need to be 100% sure you understand what they are doing for you.

If you have to implement a finalizer, follow these guidelines or have a very good reason for not doing so:

- Ensure that your finalizer executes quickly.
- Never block in your finalizer.
- Free any unmanaged resources you own.
- Don't reference any other objects.
- Don't throw any unhandled exceptions.

Dispose and Close Methods

It is generally desirable to explicitly call clean-up code once you have determined that an object will no longer be used. Microsoft recommends that you write a method named either `Dispose` or `Close` (depending on the semantics of the type) to perform the cleanup required. If you also have a destructor, include a special call to the static SuppressFinalize method on the System.GC type to indicate that the destructor no longer needs to be called. Typically, the real destructor is written to call the Dispose/Close method, as follows:

```
using System;
public class Worker : IDisposable {
  bool disposed = false;
  int id;
  public Worker(int id) {
    this.id=id;
  }
  // ...
  protected virtual void Dispose(bool disposing) {
    if (!this.disposed) { // don't dispose more than once
      if (disposing) {
        // disposing==true means you're not in the finalizer, so
        // you can reference other objects here
        Console.WriteLine("#{0}: OK to clean up other objects.", id);
      }
      Console.WriteLine("#{0}: disposing.", id);
      // Perform normal cleanup
    }
    this.disposed = true;
  }
  public void Dispose() {
    Dispose(true);
    // Mark this object finalized
    GC.SuppressFinalize(this); // no need to destruct this instance
  }
  ~Worker() {
    Dispose(false);
    Console.WriteLine("#{0}: destructing.", id);
  }
  public static void Main() {
    // create a worker and call Dispose when we're done.
    using(Worker w1 = new Worker(1)) {
      // ...
    }
    // create a worker that will get cleaned up when the CLR
    // gets around to it.
    Worker w2 = new Worker(2);
  }
}
```

If you run this code, you will see that Worker 1 is never finalized, since its Dispose() method is implicitly called (the using block guarantees this). Worker 2 is finalized and disposed when the CLR gets around to it, but it's never given a chance to clean up other objects. The disposable pattern gives you a way to close or dispose of any external objects you might be using, such as an I/O stream:

```
#1: OK to clean up other objects.
#1: disposing.
```

```
#2: disposing.
#2: destructing.
```

Interop with Native DLLs

PInvoke, short for Platform Invocation Services, lets C# access functions, structs, and callbacks in unmanaged DLLs. For example, perhaps you wish to call the MessageBox function in the Windows user32.dll:

```
int MessageBox(HWND hWnd, LPCTSTR lpText,
                    LPCTSTR lpCation, UINT uType);
```

To call this function, write a static extern method decorated with the DllImport attribute:

```
using System.Runtime.InteropServices;
class MsgBoxTest {
  [DllImport("user32.dll")]
  static extern int MessageBox(int hWnd, string text,
                              string caption, int type);
  public static void Main() {
    MessageBox(0, "Please do not press this button again.",
              "Attention", 0);
  }
}
```

PInvoke then finds and loads the required Win32 DLLs and resolves the entry point of the requested function. The CLR includes a marshaler that knows how to convert parameters and return values between .NET types and unmanaged types. In this example the int parameters translate directly to four-byte integers that the function expects, and the string parameters are converted to null-terminated arrays of characters using one-byte ANSI characters under Win9x or two-byte Unicode characters under Windows NT, 2000, and XP.

Marshaling Common Types

The CLR marshaler is a .NET facility that knows about the core types used by COM and the Windows API and provides default translations to CLR types for you. The bool type, for instance, can be translated into a two-byte Windows BOOL type or a four-byte Boolean type. You can override a default translation using the MarshalAs attribute:

```
using System.Runtime.InteropServices;
static extern int Foo([MarshalAs(UnmanagedType.LPStr)]
                      string s);
```

In this case, the marshaler was told to use LPStr, so it will always use ANSI characters. Array classes and the StringBuilder class will copy the marshaled value from an external function back to the managed value, as follows:

```
using System;
using System.Text;
using System.Runtime.InteropServices;
class Test {
  [DllImport("kernel32.dll")]
  static extern int GetWindowsDirectory(StringBuilder sb,
                                        int maxChars);

  static void Main( ) {
    StringBuilder s = new StringBuilder(256);
    GetWindowsDirectory(s, 256);
    Console.WriteLine(s);
  }
}
```

Marshaling Classes and Structs

Passing a class or struct to a C function requires marking the struct or class with the StructLayout attribute:

```
using System;
using System.Runtime.InteropServices;
[StructLayout(LayoutKind.Sequential)]
struct SystemTime {
  public ushort wYear;
  public ushort wMonth;
  public ushort wDayOfWeek;
  public ushort wDay;
  public ushort wHour;
  public ushort wMinute;
  public ushort wSecond;
  public ushort wMilliseconds;
}
class Test {
  [DllImport("kernel32.dll")]
  static extern void GetSystemTime(ref SystemTime t);
  static void Main( ) {
    SystemTime t = new SystemTime( );
    GetSystemTime(ref t);
    Console.WriteLine(t.wYear);
  }
}
```

In both C and C#, fields in an object are located at n number of bytes from the address of that object. The difference is that a C# program finds this offset by looking it up using the field name; C field names are compiled directly into offsets. For instance, in C, wDay is just a token to represent whatever is at the address of a SystemTime instance plus 24 bytes.

For access speed and future widening of a datatype, these offsets are usually in multiples of a minimum width, called the *pack size*. For .NET types, the pack size is usually set at the discretion of the runtime, but by using the StructLayout attribute, field offsets can be controlled. The default pack size when using this attribute is 8 bytes, but it can be set to 1, 2, 4, 8, or 16 bytes (pass Pack=*packsize* to the StructLayout constructor), and there are also explicit options to control individual field offsets. This lets a .NET type be passed to a C function.

In and Out Marshaling

The previous Test example works if SystemTime is a struct and t is a ref parameter, but is actually less efficient:

```
struct SystemTime {...}
static extern void GetSystemTime(ref SystemTime t);
```

This is because the marshaler must always create fresh values for external parameters, so the previous method copies t when going in to the function and then copies the marshaled t when coming out of the function. By default, pass-by-value parameters are copied in, C# ref parameters are copied in/out, and C# out parameters are copied out, but there are exceptions for the types that have custom conversions. For instance, array classes and the StringBuilder class require copying when coming out of a function, so they are in/out. It is occasionally useful to override this behavior, with the in and out attributes. For example, if an array should be read-only, the in modifier indicates to copy only the array going into the function, and not the one coming out of it:

```
static extern void Foo([in] int[] array);
```

Callbacks from Unmanaged Code

C# can not only call C functions but can also be called by C functions, using callbacks. In C# a delegate type is used in place of a function pointer:

```
class Test {
    delegate bool CallBack(int hWnd, int lParam);
    [DllImport("user32.dll")]
    static extern int EnumWindows(CallBack hWnd, int lParam);
    static bool PrintWindow(int hWnd, int lParam) {
        Console.WriteLine(hWnd);
        return true;
    }
    static void Main( ) {
        CallBack e = new CallBack(PrintWindow);
        EnumWindows(e, 0);
    }
}
```

Predefined Interop Support Attributes

The FCL provides a set of attributes you can use to mark up your objects with information used by the CLR marshaling services to alter their default marshaling behavior.

This section describes the most common attributes you will need when interoperating with native Win32 DLLs. These attributes all exist in the System.Runtime.InteropServices namespace.

DllImport attribute

Syntax:

```
[DllImport (dll-name
  [, EntryPoint=function-name]?
  [, CharSet=charset-enum]?
  [, SetLastError=true|false]?
  [, ExactSpelling=true|false]?
  [, PreserveSig=true|false]?
  [, CallingConvention=callconv-enum]?
)] (for methods)
```

The DllImport attribute annotates an external function that defines a DLL entry point. The parameters for this attribute are:

dll-name
> A string specifying the name of the DLL.

function-name
> A string specifying the function name in the DLL. This is useful if you want the name of your C# function to be different from the name of the DLL function.

charset-enum
> A CharSet enum, specifying how to marshal strings. The default value is CharSet.Auto, which converts strings to ANSI characters on Win9x and Unicode characters on Windows NT, 2000, and XP.

SetLastError
> If true, preserves the Win32 error info. The default is false.

ExactSpelling
> If true, the EntryPoint must exactly match the function. If false, name-matching heuristics are used. The default is false.

PreserveSig
> If true, the method signature is preserved exactly as it was defined. If false, an HRESULT transformation is performed.

callconv-enum

A CallingConvention enum, specifying the mode to use with the EntryPoint. The default is StdCall.

StructLayout attribute

Syntax:

```
[StructLayout(layout-enum
  [, Pack=packing-size]?
  [, CharSet=charset-enum]?
  [, Size=absolute-size])?
] (for classes, structs)
```

The StructLayout attribute specifies how the data members of a class or struct should be laid out in memory. Although this attribute is commonly used when declaring structures that are passed to or returned from native DLLs, it can also define data structures suited to file and network I/O. The parameters for this attribute are:

layout-enum

A LayoutKind enum, which can be 1) *sequential*, which lays out fields one after the next with a minimum pack size; 2) *union*, which makes all fields have an offset of 0, so long as they are value types; or 3) *explicit*, which lets each field have a custom offset.

packing-size

An int specifying whether the packing size is 1, 2, 4, 8, or 16 bytes. The default value is 8.

charset-enum

A CharSet enum, specifying how to marshal strings. The default value is CharSet.Auto, which converts strings to ANSI characters on Win9x and Unicode characters on Windows NT, 2000, and XP.

absolute-size

Specifies the size of the struct or class. This has to be at least as large as the sum of all the members.

FieldOffset attribute

Syntax:

```
[FieldOffset (byte-offset)] (for fields)
```

The FieldOffset attribute is used within a class or struct that has explicit field layout. This attribute can be applied to a field and specifies the field offset in bytes from the start of the class or struct. Note that these offsets don't have to be strictly increasing and can overlap, thus creating a union data structure.

MarshalAs attribute

Syntax:

```
[MarshalAs(unmanaged-type
  [, named-parameters])?
] (for fields, parameters, return values)
```

The MarshalAs attribute overrides the default marshaling behavior that the marshaler applies to a parameter or field. The *unmanaged-type* value is taken from the UnmanagedType enum; see the following list for the permissible values:

Bool	LPStr	VBByRefStr
I1	LPWStr	AnsiBStr
U1	LPTStr	TBStr
I2	ByValTStr	VariantBool
U2	IUnknown	FunctionPtr
I4	IDispatch	LPVoid
U4	Struct	AsAny
I8	Interface	RPrecise
U8	SafeArray	LPArray
R4	ByValArray	LPStruct
R8	SysInt	CustomMarshaler
BStr	SysUInt	NativeTypeMax
Error	Currency	

For a detailed description of how and when to use each of these enum values, as well as other legal *named-parameters*, see the .NET Framework SDK documentation.

In attribute

Syntax:

[In] *(for parameters)*

The In attribute specifies that data should be marshaled into the caller and can be combined with the Out attribute.

Out attribute

Syntax:

[Out] *(for parameters)*

The Out attribute specifies that data should be marshaled out from the called method to the caller and can be combined with the In attribute.

Interop with COM

The CLR provides support both for exposing C# objects as COM objects and for using COM objects from C#.

Binding COM and C# Objects

Interoperating between COM and C# works through either early or late binding. Early binding allows you to program with types known at compile time, while late binding forces you to program with types via dynamic discovery, using reflection on the C# side and IDispatch on the COM side.

When calling COM programs from C#, early binding works by providing metadata in the form of an assembly for the COM object and its interfaces. *TlbImp.exe* takes a COM type library and generates the equivalent metadata in an assembly. With the generated assembly, it's possible to instantiate and call methods on a COM object just as you would on any other C# object.

When calling C# programs from COM, early binding works via a type library. Both *TlbExp.exe* and *RegAsm.exe* allow you to generate a COM type library from your assembly. You can then use this type library with tools that support early binding via type libraries such as Visual Basic 6.

Exposing COM Objects to C#

When you instantiate a COM object you are actually working with a proxy known as the Runtime Callable Wrapper (RCW). The RCW is responsible for managing the lifetime requirements of the COM object and translating the methods called on it into the appropriate calls on the COM object. When the garbage collector finalizes the RCW, it releases all references to the object it was holding. For situations in which you need to release the COM object without waiting for the garbage collector to finalize the RCW, you can use the static ReleaseComObject method of the System.Runtime. InteropServices.Marshal type.

The following example demonstrates changing the friendly name of the user with MSN Instant Messenger from C# via COM Interop:

```
// SetFN.cs - compile with /r:Messenger.dll
// Run SetFN.exe <Name> to set the FriendlyName for
//    the currently logged-in user
// Run TlbImp.exe "C:\Program Files\Messenger\msmsgs.exe"
```

```
//   to create Messenger.dll
using Messenger; // COM API for MSN Instant Messenger
public class MyApp {
  public static void Main(string[] args) {
    MsgrObject mo = new MsgrObject();
    IMsgrService im = mo.Services.PrimaryService;
    im.FriendlyName = args[0];
  }
}
```

Exposing C# Objects to COM

Just as an RCW proxy wraps a COM object when you access it from C#, code that accesses a C# object as a COM object must do so through a proxy as well. When your C# object is marshaled out to COM, the runtime creates a COM Callable Wrapper (CCW). The CCW follows the same lifetime rules as other COM objects, and as long as it is alive, a CCW maintains a traceable reference to the object it wraps, which keeps the object alive when the garbage collector is run.

The following example shows how you can export both a class and an interface from C# and control the assigned Global Unique Identifiers (GUIDs) and Dispatch IDs (DISPIDs). After compiling IRunInfo and StackSnapshot you can register both using *RegAsm.exe*.

```
// IRunInfo.cs
// Compile with:
// csc /t:library IRunInfo.cs
using System;
using System.Runtime.InteropServices;
[GuidAttribute("aa6b10a2-dc4f-4a24-ae5e-90362c2142c1")]
public interface IRunInfo {
  [DispId(1)]
  string GetRunInfo();
}

// StackSnapshot.cs
// compile with: csc /t:library /r:IRunInfo.dll StackSnapshot.cs
using System;
using System.Runtime.InteropServices;
using System.Diagnostics;
[GuidAttribute("b72ccf55-88cc-4657-8577-72bd0ff767bc")]
public class StackSnapshot : IRunInfo {
  public StackSnapshot() {
    st = new StackTrace();
  }
  [DispId(1)]
  public string GetRunInfo() {
    return st.ToString();
  }
}
```

```
    private StackTrace st;
}
```

COM Mapping in C#

When you use a COM object from C#, the RCW makes a COM method look like a normal C# instance method. In COM, methods normally return an HRESULT to indicate success or failure and use an out parameter to return a value. In C#, however, methods normally return their result values and use exceptions to report errors. The RCW handles this by checking the HRESULT returned from the call to a COM method and throwing a C# exception when it finds a failure result. With a success result, the RCW returns the parameter marked as the return value in the COM method signature.

 For more information on the argument modifiers and default mappings from COM type library types to C# types, see Appendix D.

Common COM Interop Support Attributes

The FCL provides a set of attributes you can use to mark up your objects with information needed by the CLR interop services to expose managed types to the unmanaged world as COM objects.

This section describes the most common attributes you will use for this purpose. These attributes all exist in the System.Runtime.InteropServices namespace.

ComVisible attribute

Syntax:

`[ComVisible(true|false)]` *(for assemblies, classes, structs, enums, interfaces, delegates)*

When generating a type library, all public types in an assembly are exported by default. The ComVisible attribute specifies that particular public types (or even the entire assembly) should not be exposed.

DispId attribute

Syntax:

`[DispId(dispatch-id)]` *(for methods, properties, fields)*

The DispId attribute specifies the DispID assigned to a method, field, or property for access via an IDispatch interface.

ProgId attribute

Syntax:

`[ProgId(progid)]` *(for classes)*

The `ProgId` attribute specifies the COM `ProgID` to be used for your class.

Guid attribute

Syntax:

`[GuidAttribute(guid)]` *(for assemblies, modules, classes, structs, enums, interfaces, delegates)*

The `Guid` attribute specifies the COM GUID to be used for your class or interface. This attribute should be specified using its full type name to avoid clashes with the `Guid` type.

InterfaceType attribute

Syntax:

`[InterfaceType(ComInterfaceType)]` *(for interfaces)*

By default, interfaces are generated as dual interfaces in the type library, but you can use this attribute to use one of the three COM interface types (dual, dispatch, or a traditional `IUnknown`-derived interface).

ComRegisterFunction attribute

Syntax:

`[ComRegisterFunction]` *(for methods)*

Requests that *RegAsm.exe* call a method during the process of registering your assembly. If you use this attribute, you must also specify an unregistration method that reverses all the changes you made in the registration function. Use the `ComUnregisterFunction` attribute to mark that method.

Framework Class Library Overview

In Chapter 3, we focused on some of the key aspects of the .NET Framework and how to leverage them from C#. However, access to these capabilities isn't limited to C#.

Almost all the capabilities of the .NET Framework are exposed via a set of managed types known as the .NET Framework Class Library (FCL). Because these types are CLS-compliant, they are accessible from almost any .NET language. FCL types are grouped logically by namespace and are exported from a set of assemblies (DLLs) that are part of the .NET platform.

In order to work effectively in C# on the .NET platform, it is important to understand the general capabilities in the predefined class library. However, the library is far too large to cover completely in this book, as it encompasses approximately 3,540 types grouped into 124 namespaces and exported from 38 different assemblies.

Instead, in this chapter, we give an overview of the entire FCL (broken down by logical area) and provide references to relevant types and namespaces so you can explore their details in the .NET Framework SDK on your own.

Useful tools for exploring the FCL include the .NET Framework SDK documentation, the *WinCV.exe* class browser, and the *ILDasm.exe* disassembler (see Chapter 5).

Core Types

The core types are contained in the System namespace. This namespace is the heart of the FCL and contains classes, interfaces, and attributes that all other types depend on. The root of the FCL is the type Object, from which all other .NET types derive. Other fundamental types are ValueType (the base type for structs), Enum (the base type for enums), Convert (used to convert between base types), Exception (the base type for all exceptions), and the boxed versions of the predefined value types. Interfaces used throughout the FCL—such as `ICloneable`, `IComparable`, `IFormattable`, and `IConvertible`—are defined here (see "Strings" in Chapter 3). Extended types such as `DateTime`, `TimeSpan`, and `DBNull` are also available. Other classes include support for delegates (see "Delegates" in Chapter 2), basic math operations (see "Math" in Chapter 3), attributes (see "Attributes" in Chapter 2), and exception handling (see "try Statements and Exceptions" in Chapter 2).

For more information, see the `System` namespace.

Text

The FCL provides rich support for text. Important types include a `String` class for handling immutable strings, a `StringBuilder` class that provides string-handling operations with support for locale-aware comparison operations and multiple string-encoding formats (such as ASCII, Unicode, UTF-7, and UTF-8), and a set of classes that provide regular expression support (see "Regular Expressions" in Chapter 3).

For more information, see the following namespaces:

```
System.Text
System.Text.RegularExpressions
```

An important type in other namespaces is `System.String`.

Collections

The FCL provides a set of general-purpose data structures such as `Array`, `ArrayList`, `Hashtable`, `Queue`, `Stack`, `BitArray`, and more. Standardized design patterns using common base types and public interfaces allow consistent handling of collections throughout the FCL for both predefined and user-defined collection types (see "Collections" in Chapter 3).

For more information, see the following namespaces:

```
System.Collections
System.Collections.Specialized
```

An important related type in another namespace is `System.Array`.

Streams and I/O

The FCL provides good support for accessing the standard input, output, and error streams. Classes are also provided for performing binary and text file I/O, registering for notification of filesystem events, and accessing a secure user-specific storage area known as Isolated Storage.

For more information, see the following namespaces:

```
System.IO
System.IO.IsolatedStorage
```

An important related type in another namespace is `System.Console`.

Networking

The FCL provides a layered set of classes for communicating over the network using different levels of abstraction, including raw socket access; TCP, UDP, and HTTP protocol support; a high-level, request/response mechanism based on URIs and streams; and pluggable protocol handlers (see "Networking" in Chapter 3).

For more information, see the following namespaces:

```
System.Net
System.Net.Sockets
```

An important related type in another namespace is `System.IO.Stream`.

Threading

The FCL provides rich support for building multithreaded applications, including thread and thread pool management; thread-synchronization mechanisms such as monitors, mutexes, events, reader/writer locks, etc.; and access to such underlying platform features as I/O completion ports and system timers (see "Threading" in Chapter 3).

For more information, see the following namespaces:

```
System.Threading
System.Timers
```

Important related types in other namespaces include `System.Thread` and `System.ThreadStaticAttribute`.

Security

The FCL provides classes for manipulating all elements of the .NET runtime's Code Access Security model, including security policies, security principals, permission sets, and evidence. These classes also support cryptographic algorithms such as DES, 3DES, RC2, RSA, DSig, MD5, SHA1, and Base64 encoding for stream transformations.

For more information, see the following namespaces:

```
System.Security
System.Security.Cryptography
System.Security.Cryptography.X509Certificates
System.Security.Cryptography.Xml
System.Security.Permissions
System.Security.Policy
System.Security.Principal
```

Reflection and Metadata

The .NET runtime depends heavily on the existence of metadata and the ability to inspect and manipulate it dynamically. The FCL exposes this via a set of abstract classes that mirror the significant elements of an application (assemblies, modules, types, and members) and provide support for creating instances of FCL types and new types on the fly (see "Reflection" in Chapter 3).

For more information, see the following namespaces:

```
System.Reflection
System.Reflection.Emit
```

Important related types in other namespaces include System.Type, System.Activator and System.AppDomain.

Assemblies

The FCL provides attributes that tag the metadata on an assembly with information such as target OS and processor, assembly version, and other information. The FCL also provides classes to manipulate assemblies, modules, and assembly strong names.

For more information, see the following namespace:

```
System.Reflection
```

Serialization

The FCL includes support for serializing arbitrary object graphs to and from a stream. This serialization can store and transmit complex data structures via files or the network. The default serializers provide binary and XML-based formatting but can be extended with user-defined formatters.

For more information, see the following namespaces:

```
System.Runtime.Serialization
```

```
System.Runtime.Serialization.Formatters
System.Runtime.Serialization.Formatters.Soap
System.Runtime.Serialization.Formatters.Binary
```

Important related types in other namespaces include `System.Non-SerializedAttribute` and `System.SerializableAttribute`.

Remoting

Remoting is the cornerstone of a distributed application, and the FCL provides excellent support for making and receiving remote method calls. Calls may be synchronous or asynchronous; support request/response or one-way modes; can be delivered over multiple transports (such as TCP, HTTP, and SMTP); and can be serialized in multiple formats (such as SOAP and binary). The remoting infrastructure supports multiple activation models, lease-based object lifetimes, distributed object identity, object marshaling by reference and by value, and message interception. These types can be extended with user-defined channels, serializers, proxies, and call context.

For more information, see the following namespaces:

```
System.Runtime.Remoting
System.Runtime.Remoting.Activation
System.Runtime.Remoting.Channels
System.Runtime.Remoting.Channels.Http
System.Runtime.Remoting.Channels.Tcp
System.Runtime.Remoting.Contexts
System.Runtime.Remoting.Lifetime
System.Runtime.Remoting.Messaging
System.Runtime.Remoting.Metadata
System.Runtime.Remoting.MetadataServices
System.Runtime.Remoting.Proxies
System.Runtime.Remoting.Services
```

Important related types in other namespaces include `System.AppDomain`, `System.ContextBoundObject`, `System.ContextStaticAttribute`, and `System.MarshalByRefObject`.

Web Services

Logically, web services are simply an instance of remoting. In reality, the FCL support for web services is considered part of ASP.NET and is largely separate from the CLR remoting infrastructure. Classes and attributes exist for describing and publishing web services, discovering which web services are exposed at a particular endpoint (URI), and invoking a web service method.

For more information, see the following namespaces:

```
System.Web.Services
System.Web.Services.Configuration
System.Web.Services.Description
System.Web.Services.Discovery
System.Web.Services.Protocols
```

Data Access

The FCL includes a set of classes that access data sources and manage complex data sets. Known as ADO.NET, these classes are the managed replacement for ADO under Win32. ADO.NET supports both connected and disconnected operations, multiple data providers (including nonrelational data sources), and serialization to and from XML.

For more information, see the following namespaces:

```
System.Data
System.Data.Common
System.Data.OleDb
System.Data.SqlClient
System.Data.SqlTypes
```

XML

The FCL provides broad support for XML 1.0, XML schemas, and XML namespaces, with two separate XML parsing models (a DOM2-based model and a pull-mode variant of SAX2) and implementations of XSL/T, XPath, and SOAP 1.1.

For more information, see the following namespaces:

```
System.Xml
System.Xml.Schema
System.Xml.Serialization
System.Xml.XPath
System.Xml.Xsl
```

Graphics

The FCL includes classes to support working with graphic images. Known as GDI+, these classes are the managed equivalent of GDI under Win32 and include support for brushes, fonts, bitmaps, text rendering, drawing primitives, image conversions, and print-preview capabilities.

For more information, see the following namespaces:

```
System.Drawing
System.Drawing.Design
System.Drawing.Drawing2D
System.Drawing.Imaging
System.Drawing.Printing
System.Drawing.Text
```

Rich Client Applications

The FCL includes support for creating classic GUI applications. This support is called Windows Forms and consists of a forms package, a predefined set of GUI components, and a component model suited to RAD designer tools. These classes provide varying degrees of abstraction from low-level, message-loop handler classes to high-level layout managers and visual inheritance.

For more information, see the following namespaces:

```
System.Windows.Forms
System.Windows.Forms.Design
```

Web-Based Applications

The FCL includes support for creating web-based applications. This support is called *Web Forms* and consists of a server-side forms package that generates HTML UI, a predefined set of HTML-based GUI widgets, and a component model suited to RAD designer tools. The FCL also includes a set of classes that manage session state, security, caching, debugging, tracing, localization, configuration, and deployment for web-based applications. Finally, the FCL includes the classes and attributes that produce and consume web services, which were described previously in "Web Services." Collectively, these capabilities are known as ASP.NET and are a complete replacement for ASP under Win32.

For more information, see the following namespaces:

```
System.Web
System.Web.Caching
System.Web.Configuration
System.Web.Hosting
System.Web.Mail
System.Web.Security
System.Web.SessionState
System.Web.UI
System.Web.UI.Design
System.Web.UI.Design.WebControls
System.Web.UI.HtmlControls
```

```
System.Web.UI.WebControls
```

Globalization

The FCL provides classes that aid globalization by supporting code-page conversions, locale-aware string operations, date/time conversions, and the use of resource files to centralize localization work.

For more information, see the following namespaces:

```
System.Globalization
System.Resources
```

Configuration

The FCL provides access to the .NET configuration system, which includes a per-user and per-application configuration model with inheritance of configuration settings, and a transacted installer framework. Classes exist both to use the configuration framework and to extend it.

For more information, see the following namespaces:

```
System.Configuration
System.Configuration.Assemblies
System.Configuration.Install
```

Advanced Component Services

The FCL provides support for building on the COM+ services such as distributed transactions, JIT activation, object pooling, queuing, and events. The FCL also includes types that provide access to reliable, asynchronous, one-way messaging via an existing Message Queue infrastructure (MSMQ). The FCL also includes classes that provide access to existing directory services (Active Directory).

For more information, see the following namespaces:

```
System.DirectoryServices
System.EnterpriseServices
System.EnterpriseServices.CompensatingResourceManager
System.Messaging
```

Diagnostics and Debugging

The FCL includes classes that provide debug tracing with multilistener support; access to the event log; access to process, thread, and stack frame information; and the ability to create and consume performance counters.

For more information, see the following namespaces:

```
System.Diagnostics
System.Diagnostics.SymbolStore
```

Interoperating with Unmanaged Code

The .NET runtime supports bidirectional interop with unmanaged code via COM, COM+, and native Win32 API calls. The FCL provides a set of classes and attributes that support this, including precise control of managed-object lifetime and the option of creating user-defined custom marshalers to handle specific interop situations.

For more information, see the following namespaces:

```
System.Runtime.InteropServices
System.Runtime.InteropServices.CustomMarshalers
System.Runtime.InteropServices.Expando
```

Important types in other namespaces include System.Buffer.

Compiler and Tool Support

In the .NET runtime, components are distinguished from classes by the presence of additional metadata and other apparatus that facilitate the use of component forms packages such as Windows Forms and Web Forms. The FCL provides classes and attributes that support both the creation of components and the creation of tools that consume components. These classes also include the ability to generate and compile C#, JScript, and VB.NET source code.

For more information, see the following namespaces:

```
Microsoft.CSharp
Microsoft.JScript
Microsoft.VisualBasic
Microsoft.Vsa
System.CodeDom
System.CodeDom.Compiler
System.ComponentModel
System.ComponentModel.Design
System.ComponentModel.Design.Serialization
System.Runtime.CompilerServices
```

Runtime Facilities

The FCL provides classes that can control runtime behavior. The canonical examples are the classes that control the garbage collector and those that provide strong and weak reference support.

For more information, see the following namespace:

```
System
```

An important related type in another namespace is `System.Runtime.InteropServices.GCHandle`.

Native OS Facilities

The FCL provides support for controlling existing NT services and creating new ones. It also provides access to certain native Win32 facilities such as the Windows registry and the Windows Management Instrumentation (WMI).

For more information, see the following namespaces:

```
Microsoft.Win32
System.Management
System.Management.Instrumentation
System.ServiceProcess
```

Undocumented Types

The assemblies that make up the .NET Framework also export many types and namespaces that are not documented. These types and namespaces generally represent either implementation details that are subject to change, vestigial code from earlier betas, or tool-specific code that happens to be managed and is therefore subject to examination via reflection. Regardless of the reason, one cannot count on undocumented types, nor expect any support from Microsoft.

That said, there is useful information to be gained from investigating these private implementation details. Examples of this include: programmatic access to the GAC; predefined Win32 structures and COM interfaces, such as internals of SoapSuds.exe, RegAsm.exe, TlbImp.exe and TlbExp.exe; and browser, tool and OS integration helpers.

Many of the documented namespaces include additional undocumented types. Additionally, the following namespaces are completely undocumented:

```
Accessibility
IEHost.Execute
Microsoft.CLRAdmin
Microsoft.IE
Microsoft.JScript.Vsa
Microsoft.VisualBasic.CompilerServices
Microsoft.VisualBasic.Vsa
Microsoft.VisualC
Microsoft_VsaVb
RegCode
SoapSudsCode
System.Diagnostics.Design
System.EnterpriseServices.Internal
System.Messaging.Design
System.Runtime.Remoting.Metadata.W3cXsd2001
System.ServiceProcess.Design
System.Web.Handlers
System.Web.RegularExpressions
System.Web.Services.Configuration
System.Web.Util
System.Windows.Forms.ComponentModel.Com2Interop
System.Windows.Forms.PropertyGridInternal
TlbExpCode
TlbImpCode
```

To investigate these types and namespaces, use ILDasm.exe to examine the metadata and MSIL.

Essential .NET Tools

The .NET Framework SDK contains many useful programming tools. Here, in an alphabetical list, are those we have found most useful or necessary for developing C# applications. Unless otherwise noted, the tools in this list can be found either in the \bin directory of your .NET Framework SDK installation or in the *%SystemRoot%\Microsoft.NET\Framework\VERSION* directory (replace *VERSION* with the framework version). Once the .NET Framework is installed, you can access these tools from any directory. To use any of these tools, invoke a Command Prompt window and enter the name of the desired tool. For a complete list of the available command-line switches for any given tool, enter the tool name (e.g., csc) and press the Return or Enter key.

ADepends.exe: assembly dependency list
> *Adepends* displays all assemblies that a given assembly is dependent on to load. This is a useful C# program found among the samples in the *Tool Developers Guide* directory beneath the .NET Framework or Visual Studio .NET directory tree. You need to install these samples before you can use them, because they are not installed by default.

Al.exe: assembly linking utility
> Creates an assembly manifest from the modules and resources files you name. You can also include Win32 resources files. Here's an example:
>
> ```
> al /out:c.dll a.netmodule b.netmodule
> ```

CorDbg.exe: runtime debugger
> General source-level, command-line debug utility for MSIL programs. Very useful tool for C# source debugging. Source for *cordbg* is available in the *Tool Developers Guide* directory.

Csc.exe: C# compiler
> Compiles C# sources and incorporates resource files and separately compiled modules. Also allows you to specify conditional compilation

options, XML documentation, and path information. Here are some examples:

```
csc foo.cs /r:bar.dll /win32res:foo.res
csc foo.cs /debug /define:TEMP
```

DbgClr.exe: GUI debugger

Windows-based, source-level debugger. Available in the *GuiDebug* directory of the .NET Framework SDK installation.

GACUtil.exe: global assembly cache utility

Allows you to install, uninstall, and list the contents of the global assembly cache. Here's an example:

```
gacutil /i c.dll
```

ILAsm.exe: MSIL assembler

Creates MSIL modules and assemblies directly from an MSIL textual representation.

ILDasm.exe: MSIL disassembler

Disassembles modules and assemblies. The default is to display a tree-style representation, but you can also specify an output file. Here are some examples:

```
ildasm b.dll
ildasm b.dll /out=b.asm
```

InstallUtil.exe: installer utility

Executes installers and uninstallers contained within the assembly. A logfile can be written, and state information can be persisted.

Ngen.exe: native image generator

Compiles an assembly to native code and installs a native image in the local assembly cache. That native image is used each time you access the original assembly, even though the original assembly contains MSIL. If the runtime can't locate the native image, it falls back on JIT compilation. Here are some examples:

```
ngen foo.exe
ngen foo.dll
```

nmake.exe: make utility

Common utility that scripts building of multiple components and source files and tracks rebuild dependency information. See Appendix E for more information.

PEVerify.exe: portable executable verifier

Verifies that your compiler has generated type-safe MSIL. C# will always generate type-safe MSIL. Useful interop with ILASM-based programs.

RegAsm.exe: register assembly tool

Registers an assembly in the system registry. This allows COM clients to call managed methods. You can also use it to generate the registry file for future registration. Here's an example:

```
regasm /regfile:c.reg c.dll
```

RegSvcs.exe: register services utility

Registers an assembly to COM+ 1.0, and installs its typelib into an existing application. Can also generate a typelib. Here's an example:

```
regsvcs foo.dll /appname:comapp /tlb:newfoo.tlb
```

Sn.exe: shared name utility

Verifies assemblies and their key information. Also generates key files. Here's an example:

```
sn -k mykey.snk
```

SoapSuds.exe: SoapSuds utility

Creates XML schemas for services in an assembly and creates assemblies from a schema. You can also reference the schema via its URL. Here's an example:

```
soapsuds
    -url:http://localhost/myapp/app.soap?wsdl
    -os:app.xml
```

TlbExp.exe: type library exporter

Exports a COM typelib derived from the public types within the supplied assembly. Differs from *regasm* in that it doesn't perform any registration. Here's an example:

```
tlbexp /out:c.tlb c.dll
```

TlbImp.exe: type library importer

Creates a managed assembly from the supplied COM typelib, mapping the type definitions to .NET types. You need to import this new assembly into your C# program for use. Here's an example:

```
tlbimp /out:MyOldCom.dll MyCom.tlb
```

Wsdl.exe: web services description language tool

Creates service descriptions and generates proxies for ASP.NET web-service methods. See the ASP.NET documentation in the .NET Framework SDK for more detail on web services.

WinCV.exe: windows class viewer

Searches for matching names within a supplied assembly. If none are supplied, it uses the default libraries. The namespaces and classes are displayed in a listbox, and the selected type information is displayed in another window.

Xsd.exe: XML schema definition tool

Generates XML schemas from XDR, XML files, or class information. Can also generate DataSet or class information from a schema. Here's an example:

```
xsd foo.xdr
xsd bar.dll
```

C# Keywords

abstract
> A class modifier that specifies that the class must be derived-from to be instantiated.

as
> A binary operator type that casts the left operand to the type specified by the right operand and that returns null rather than throwing an exception if the cast fails.

base
> A variable with the same meaning as this, except that it accesses a base-class implementation of a member.

bool
> A logical datatype that can be true or false.

break
> A jump statement that exits a loop or switch statement block.

byte
> A one-byte, unsigned integral data type.

case
> A selection statement that defines a particular choice in a switch statement.

catch
> The part of a try statement that catches exceptions of a specific type defined in the catch clause.

char
> A two-byte, Unicode character data type.

checked
> A statement or operator that enforces arithmetic bounds checking on an expression or statement block.

class

An extendable reference type that combines data and functionality into one unit.

const

A modifier for a local variable or field declaration that indicates that the value is a constant. A const is evaluated at compile time and can be only a predefined type.

continue

A jump statement that skips the remaining statements in a statement block and continues to the next iteration in a loop.

decimal

A 16-byte precise decimal datatype.

default

A marker in a switch statement specifying the action to take when no case statements match the switch expression.

delegate

A type for defining a method signature so delegate instances can hold and invoke a method or list of methods that match its signature.

do

A loop statement to iterate a statement block until an expression at the end of the loop evaluates to false.

double

An eight-byte, floating-point data type.

else

A conditional statement that defines the action to take when a preceding if expression evaluates to false.

enum

A value type that defines a group of named numeric constants.

event

A member modifier for a delegate field or property that indicates that only the += and -= methods of the delegate can be accessed.

explicit

An operator that defines an explicit conversion.

extern

A method modifier that indicates that the method is implemented with unmanaged code.

false

A Boolean literal.

finally

    The part of a try statement to execute whenever control leaves the scope of the try block.

fixed

    A statement to pin down a reference type so the garbage collector won't move it during pointer arithmetic operations.

float

    A four-byte floating-point data type.

for

    A loop statement that combines an initialization statement, continuation condition, and iterative statement into one statement.

foreach

    A loop statement that iterates over collections that implement IEnumerable.

get

    The name of the accessor that returns the value of a property.

goto

    A jump statement that jumps to a label within the same method and same scope as the jump point.

if

    A conditional statement that executes its statement block if its expression evaluates to true.

implicit

    An operator that defines an implicit conversion.

in

    The operator between a type and an IEnumerable in a foreach statement.

int

    A four-byte, signed integral data type.

interface

    A contract that specifies the members that a class or struct may implement to receive generic services for that type.

internal

    An access modifier that indicates that a type or type member is accessible only to other types in the same assembly.

is

    A relational operator that evaluates to true if the left operand's type matches, is derived-from, or implements the type specified by the right operand.

lock
A statement that acquires a lock on a reference-type object to help multiple threads cooperate.

long
An eight-byte, signed integral data type.

namespace
A keyword that maps a set of types to a common name.

new
An operator that calls a constructor on a type, allocating a new object on the heap if the type is a reference type, or initializing the object if the type is a value type. The keyword is overloaded to hide an inherited member.

null
A reference-type literal that indicates that no object is referenced.

object
The type all other types derive from.

operator
A method modifier that overloads operators.

out
A parameter modifier that specifies that the parameter is passed by reference and must be assigned by the method being called.

override
A method modifier that indicates that a method of a class overrides a virtual method of a class or interface.

params
A parameter modifier that specifies that the last parameter of a method may accept multiple parameters of the same type.

private
An access modifier that indicates that only the containing type can access the member.

protected
An access modifier that indicates that only the containing type or derived types can access the member.

public
An access modifier that indicates that a type or type member is accessible to all other types.

readonly
A field modifier specifying that a field can be assigned only once, either in its declaration or in its containing type's constructor.

ref

> A parameter modifier that specifies that the parameter is passed by reference and is assigned before being passed to the method.

return

> A jump statement that exits a method, specifying a return value when the method is non-void.

sbyte

> A one-byte, signed integral data type.

sealed

> A class modifier that indicates a class cannot be derived-from.

set

> The name of the accessor that sets the value of a property.

short

> A two-byte, signed integral data type.

sizeof

> An operator that returns the size in bytes of a struct.

stackalloc

> An operator that returns a pointer to a specified number of value types allocated on the stack.

static

> A type member modifier that indicates that the member applies to the type rather than to an instance of the type.

string

> A predefined reference type that represents an immutable sequence of Unicode characters.

struct

> A value type that combines data and functionality in one unit.

switch

> A selection statement that allows a selection of choices to be made based on the value of a predefined type.

this

> A variable that references the current instance of a class or struct.

throw

> A jump statement that throws an exception when an abnormal condition has occurred.

true

> A Boolean literal.

try
> A statement that provides a way to handle an exception or a premature exit in a statement block.

typeof
> An operator that returns the type of an object as a System.Type object.

uint
> A four-byte, unsigned integral data type.

ulong
> An eight-byte, unsigned integral data type.

unchecked
> A statement or operator that prevents arithmetic bounds checking on an expression.

unsafe
> A method modifier or statement that permits pointer arithmetic to be performed within a particular block.

ushort
> A two-byte, unsigned integral data type.

using
> A directive that specifies that types in a particular namespace can be referred to without requiring their fully qualified type names. The keyword is overloaded as a statement that allows an object that implements IDisposable to be disposed of at the end of the statement's scope.

value
> The name of the implicit variable set by the set accessor of a property.

virtual
> A class method modifier that indicates that a method can be overridden by a derived class.

void
> A keyword used in place of a type for methods that don't have a return value.

volatile
> A field modifier indicating that a field's value may be modified in a multithreaded scenario and that neither the compiler nor runtime should perform optimizations with that field.

while
> A loop statement to iterate a statement block while an expression at the start of each iteration evaluates to false.

Regular Expressions

The following tables summarize the regular expression grammar and syntax supported by the regular expression classes in System.Text.RegularExpressions. Each of the modifiers and qualifiers in the tables can substantially change the behavior of the matching and searching patterns. For further information on regular expressions, we recommend the definitive *Mastering Regular Expressions* by Jeffrey E. F. Friedl (O'Reilly).

All the syntax described in Table B-1 through Table B-10 should match the Perl5 syntax, with specific exceptions noted.

Table B-1. Character escapes

Escape Code Sequence	Meaning	Hexadecimal equivalent
\a	Bell	\u0007
\b	Backspace	\u0008
\t	Tab	\u0009
\r	Carriage return	\u000D
\v	Vertical tab	\u000B
\f	Form feed	\u000C
\n	Newline	\u000A
\e	Escape	\u001B
\040	ASCII character as octal	
\x20	ASCII character as hex	
\cC	ASCII control character	
\u0020	Unicode character as hex	
\non-escape	A nonescape character	

Special case: within a regular expression, \b means word boundary, except in a [] set, in which \b means the backspace character.

Table B-2. Substitutions

Expression	Meaning
$group-number	Substitutes last substring matched by group-number
${group-name}	Substitutes last substring matched by (?<group-name>)
$$	Substitutes a literal "$"
$&	Substitutes copy of the entire match
$'	Substitutes text of the input string preceding match
$'	Substitutes text of the input string following match
$+	Substitutes the last captures group
$_	Substitutes the entire input string

Substitutions are specified only within a replacement pattern.

Table B-3. Character sets

Expression	Meaning
.	Matches any character except \n
[characterlist]	Matches a single character in the list
[^characterlist]	Matches a single character not in the list
[char0-char1]	Matches a single character in a range
\w	Matches a word character; same as [a-zA-Z_0-9]
\W	Matches a nonword character
\s	Matches a space character; same as [\n\r\t\v\f]
\S	Matches a nonspace character
\d	Matches a decimal digit; same as [0-9]
\D	Matches a nondigit

Table B-4. Positioning assertions

Expression	Meaning
^	Beginning of line
$	End of line
\A	Beginning of string
\Z	End of line or string
\z	Exactly the end of string
\G	Where search started
\b	On a word boundary
\B	Not on a word boundary

Table B-5. Quantifiers

Quantifier	Meaning
*	0 or more matches
+	1 or more matches
?	0 or 1 matches
{n}	Exactly n matches
{n,}	At least n matches
{n,m}	At least n, but no more than m matches
*?	Lazy *, finds first match that has minimum repeats
+?	Lazy +, minimum repeats, but at least 1
??	Lazy ?, zero or minimum repeats
{n}?	Lazy {n}, exactly n matches
{n,}?	Lazy {n}, minimum repeats, but at least n
{n,m}?	Lazy {n,m}, minimum repeats, but at least n, and no more than m

Table B-6. Grouping constructs

Syntax	Meaning
( )	Capture matched substring
(?<name>)	Capture matched substring into group name[a]
(?<number>)	Capture matched substring into group number[a]
(?<name1-name2>)	Undefine name2 and store interval and current group into name1; if name2 is undefined, matching backtracks; name1 is optional[a]
(?:)	Noncapturing group
(?imnsx-imnsx:)	Apply or disable matching options
(?=)	Continue matching only if subexpression matches on right[c]
(?!)	Continue matching only if subexpression doesn't match on right[c]
(?<=)	Continue matching only if subexpression matches on left[bc]
(?<!)	Continue matching only if subexpression doesn't match on left[bc]
(?>)	Subexpression is matched once, but isn't backtracked

[a] Single quotes may be used instead of angle brackets, for example (?'name').
[b] This construct doesn't backtrack; this is to remain compatible with Perl5.
[c] Zero-width assertion; does not consume any characters.

> The named capturing group syntax follows a suggestion made by Jeffrey Friedl in *Mastering Regular Expressions* (O'Reilly). All other grouping constructs use the Perl5 syntax.

Table B-7. Back references

Parameter syntax	Meaning
\count	Back reference *count* occurrences
\k<*name*>	Named back reference

Table B-8. Alternation

Expression syntax	Meaning
|	Logical OR
(?(*expression*)yes|no)	Matches yes if expression matches, else no; the no is optional
(?(*name*)yes|no)	Matches yes if named string has a match, else no; the no is optional

Table B-9. Miscellaneous constructs

Expression syntax	Meaning
(?*imnsx-imnsx*)	Set or disable options in midpattern
(?#)	Inline comment
# [*to end of line*]	X-mode comment (requires x option or IgnorePatternWhitespace)

Table B-10. Regular expression options

Option	RegexOption value	Meaning
i	IgnoreCase	Case-insensitive match
m	MultiLine	Multiline mode; changes ^ and $ so they match beginning and ending of any line
n	ExplicitCapture	Capture explicitly named or numbered groups
	Compiled	Compile to MSIL
s	SingleLine	Single-line mode; changes meaning of " . " so it matches every character
x	IgnorePatternWhitespace	Eliminates unescaped whitespace from the pattern
	RightToLeft	Search from right to left; can't be specified in midstream

Format Specifiers

Table C-1 lists the numeric format specifiers supported by the ToString method on the predefined numeric types (see Chapter 3).

Table C-1. Numeric format specifiers

Specifier	String result	Data type
C[*n*]	$XX,XX.XX	Currency
	($XX,XXX.XX)	
D[*n*]	[-]XXXXXXX	Decimal
E[*n*] or e[*n*]	[-]X.XXXXXXE+xxx	Exponent
	[-]X.XXXXXXe+xxx	
	[-]X.XXXXXXE-xxx	
	[-]X.XXXXXXe-xxx	
F[*n*]	[-]XXXXXXX.XX	Fixed point
G[*n*]	General or scientific	General
N[*n*]	[-]XX,XXX.XX	Number
P[*n*]	[-]XX,XXX.XX %	Percent
R	Round-trip format	Floating point
X[*n*] or x[*n*]	Hex representation	Hex

This is an example that uses numeric format specifiers without precision specifiers:

```
using System;
class TestDefaultFormats {
  static void Main() {
    int i = 654321;
    Console.WriteLine("{0:C}", i); // $654,321.00
    Console.WriteLine("{0:D}", i); // 654321
    Console.WriteLine("{0:E}", i); // 6.543210E+005
    Console.WriteLine("{0:F}", i); // 654321.00
```

```
        Console.WriteLine("{0:G}", i); // 654321
        Console.WriteLine("{0:N}", i); // 654,321.00
        Console.WriteLine("{0:P}", i); // 65,432,100.00 %
        Console.WriteLine("{0:P}", .42); // 42.00 %
        Console.WriteLine("{0:X}", i); // 9FBF1
        Console.WriteLine("{0:x}", i); // 9fbf1
        // Round-trip conversions
        string s1 = Math.PI.ToString("G");
        Console.WriteLine(s1); // 3.14159265358979
        string s2 = Math.PI.ToString("R");
        Console.WriteLine(s2); // 3.1415926535897931
        Console.WriteLine(Math.PI == Double.Parse(s1)); // False
        Console.WriteLine(Math.PI == Double.Parse(s2)); // True
    }
}
```

This is an example that uses numeric format specifiers with precision specifiers on a variety of int values:

```
using System;
class TestIntegerFormats {
  static void Main( ) {
    int i = 123;
    Console.WriteLine("{0:C6}", i); // $123.000000
    Console.WriteLine("{0:D6}", i); // 000123
    Console.WriteLine("{0:E6}", i); // 1.230000E+002
    Console.WriteLine("{0:G6}", i); // 123
    Console.WriteLine("{0:N6}", i); // 123.000000
    Console.WriteLine("{0:P6}", i); // 12,300.000000 %
    Console.WriteLine("{0:X6}", i); // 00007B
    i = -123;
    Console.WriteLine("{0:C6}", i); // ($123.000000)
    Console.WriteLine("{0:D6}", i); // -000123
    Console.WriteLine("{0:E6}", i); // -1.230000E+002
    Console.WriteLine("{0:G6}", i); // -123
    Console.WriteLine("{0:N6}", i); // -123.000000
    Console.WriteLine("{0:P6}", i); // -12,300.000000 %
    Console.WriteLine("{0:X6}", i); // FFFF85
    i = 0;
    Console.WriteLine("{0:C6}", i); // $0.000000
    Console.WriteLine("{0:D6}", i); // 000000
    Console.WriteLine("{0:E6}", i); // 0.000000E+000
    Console.WriteLine("{0:G6}", i); // 0
    Console.WriteLine("{0:N6}", i); // 0.000000
    Console.WriteLine("{0:P6}", i); // 0.000000 %
    Console.WriteLine("{0:X6}", i); // 000000
  }
}
```

Here's an example that uses numeric format specifiers with precision specifiers on a variety of double values:

```
using System;
class TestDoubleFormats {
```

```
static void Main( ) {
  double d = 1.23;
  Console.WriteLine("{0:C6}", d); // $1.230000
  Console.WriteLine("{0:E6}", d); // 1.230000E+000
  Console.WriteLine("{0:G6}", d); // 1.23
  Console.WriteLine("{0:N6}", d); // 1.230000
  Console.WriteLine("{0:P6}", d); // 123.000000 %
  d = -1.23;
  Console.WriteLine("{0:C6}", d); // ($1.230000)
  Console.WriteLine("{0:E6}", d); // -1.230000E+000
  Console.WriteLine("{0:G6}", d); // -1.23
  Console.WriteLine("{0:N6}", d); // -1.230000
  Console.WriteLine("{0:P6}", d); // -123.000000 %
  d = 0;
  Console.WriteLine("{0:C6}", d); // $0.000000
  Console.WriteLine("{0:E6}", d); // 0.000000E+000
  Console.WriteLine("{0:G6}", d); // 0
  Console.WriteLine("{0:N6}", d); // 0.000000
  Console.WriteLine("{0:P6}", d); // 0.000000 %
  }
}
```

Picture Format Specifiers

Table C-2 lists the valid picture format specifiers supported by the ToString method on the predefined numeric types (see the documentation for System. IFormattable in the .NET SDK). The picture format can include up to three sections separated by a semicolon. With one section, the format specifier is applied to all values. With two sections, the first format specifier applies to zero and positive values, and the second applies to negative values. With three sections, the first specifier applies to positive values, the second applies to negative values, and the third applies to zero.

Table C-2. Picture format specifiers

Specifier	String result
0	Zero placeholder
#	Digit placeholder
.	Decimal point
,	Group separator or multiplier
%	Percent notation
E0, E+0, E-0, e0 e+0, e-0	Exponent notation
\	Literal character quote
'xx' "xx"	Literal string quote
;	Section separator

Here's an example using picture format specifiers on some int values:

```
using System;
class TestIntegerCustomFormats {
  static void Main( ) {
    int i = 123;
    Console.WriteLine("{0:#0}", i);                 // 123
    Console.WriteLine("{0:#0;(#0)}", i);            // Two sections: 123
    Console.WriteLine("{0:#0;(#0);<zero>}", i);     // Three sections: 123
    Console.WriteLine("{0:#%}", i);                 // 12300%
    i = -123;
    Console.WriteLine("{0:#0}", i);                 // -123
    Console.WriteLine("{0:#0;(#0)}", i);            // Two sections: (123)
    Console.WriteLine("{0:#0;(#0);<zero>}", i);     // Three sections: (123)
    Console.WriteLine("{0:#%}", i);                 // -12300%
    i = 0;
    Console.WriteLine("{0:#0}", i);                 // 0
    Console.WriteLine("{0:#0;(#0)}", i);            // Two sections: 0
    Console.WriteLine("{0:#0;(#0);<zero>}", i);     // Three sections: <zero>
    Console.WriteLine("{0:#%}", i);                 // %
  }
}
```

The following is an example that uses these picture format specifiers on a variety of double values:

```
using System;
class TestDoubleCustomFormats {
  static void Main( ) {
    double d = 1.23;
    Console.WriteLine("{0:#.000E+00}", d);          // 1.230E+00
    Console.WriteLine(
      "{0:#.000E+00;(#.000E+00)}", d);              // 1.230E+00
    Console.WriteLine(
      "{0:#.000E+00;(#.000E+00);<zero>}", d);       // 1.230E+00
    Console.WriteLine("{0:#%}", d);                 // 123%
    d = -1.23;
    Console.WriteLine("{0:#.000E+00}", d);          // -1.230E+00
    Console.WriteLine(
      "{0:#.000E+00;(#.000E+00)}", d);              // (1.230E+00)
    Console.WriteLine(
      "{0:#.000E+00;(#.000E+00);<zero>}", d);       // (1.230E+00)
    Console.WriteLine("{0:#%}", d);                 // -123%
    d = 0;
    Console.WriteLine("{0:#.000E+00}", d);          // 0.000E+01
    Console.WriteLine(
      "{0:#.000E+00;(#.000E+00)}", d);              // 0.000E+01
    Console.WriteLine(
      "{0:#.000E+00;(#.000E+00);<zero>}", d);       // <zero>
    Console.WriteLine("{0:#%}", d);                 // %
  }
}
```

DateTime Format Specifiers

Table C-3 lists the valid format specifiers supported by the Format method on the DateTime type (see System.IFormattable).

Table C-3. DateTime format specifiers

Specifier	String result
d	MM/dd/yyyy
D	dddd, MMMM dd, yyyy
f	dddd, MMMM dd, yyyy HH:mm
F	dddd, MMMM dd, yyyy HH:mm:ss
g	MM/dd/yyyy HH:mm
G	MM/dd/yyyy HH:mm:ss
m, M	MMMM dd
r, R	Ddd, dd MMM yyyy HH:mm:ss GMT
s	yyyy-MM-ddTHH:mm:ss
t	HH:mm
T	HH:mm:ss
u	yyyy-MM-dd HH:mm:ssZ
U	dddd, MMMM dd, yyyy HH:mm:ss
y, Y	MMMM, yyyy

Here's an example that uses these custom format specifiers on a DateTime value:

```
using System;
class TestDateTimeFormats {
  static void Main( ) {
    DateTime dt = new DateTime(2000, 10, 11, 15, 32, 14);

    // Prints "10/11/2000 3:32:14 PM"
    Console.WriteLine(dt.ToString( ));
    // Prints "10/11/2000 3:32:14 PM"
    Console.WriteLine("{0}", dt);
    // Prints "10/11/2000"
    Console.WriteLine("{0:d}", dt);

    // Prints "Wednesday, October 11, 2000"
    Console.WriteLine("{0:D}", dt);
    // Prints "Wednesday, October 11, 2000 3:32 PM"
    Console.WriteLine("{0:f}", dt);
    // Prints "Wednesday, October 11, 2000 3:32:14 PM"
    Console.WriteLine("{0:F}", dt);

    // Prints "10/11/2000 3:32 PM"
    Console.WriteLine("{0:g}", dt);
```

```
// Prints "10/11/2000 3:32:14 PM"
Console.WriteLine("{0:G}", dt);

// Prints "October 11"
Console.WriteLine("{0:m}", dt);
// Prints "October 11"
Console.WriteLine("{0:M}", dt);

// Prints "Wed, 11 Oct 2000 15:32:14 GMT"
Console.WriteLine("{0:r}", dt);
// Prints "Wed, 11 Oct 2000 15:32:14 GMT"
Console.WriteLine("{0:R}", dt);

// Prints "3:32 PM"
Console.WriteLine("{0:t}", dt);
// Prints "3:32:14 PM"
Console.WriteLine("{0:T}", dt);

// Prints "2000-10-11T15:32:14"
Console.WriteLine("{0:s}", dt);
// Prints "2000-10-11 15:32:14Z"
Console.WriteLine("{0:u}", dt);
// Prints "Wednesday, October 11, 2000 7:32:14 PM"
Console.WriteLine("{0:U}", dt);

// Prints "October, 2000"
Console.WriteLine("{0:y}", dt);
// Prints "October, 2000"
Console.WriteLine("{0:Y}", dt);
// Prints "Wednesday the 11 day of October in the year 2000"
Console.WriteLine(
    "{0:dddd 'the' d 'day of' MMMM 'in the year' yyyy}", dt);
  }
}
```

Data Marshaling

When calling between the runtime environment and existing COM interfaces, the CLR performs automatic data marshaling for CLR types into compatible COM types.

Table D-1 describes the C# to COM default data type mapping.

Table D-1. C# type to COM type mapping

C# type	COM type
bool	VARIANT_BOOL
char	unsigned short
sbyte	char
byte	unsigned char
short	short
ushort	unsigned short
int	int
uint	unsigned int
long	hyper
ulong	unsigned hyper
float	float
double	double
decimal	DECIMAL
object	VARIANT, IUnknown*, IDispatch*
string	BSTR
System.DateTime	DATE[a]
System.Guid	GUID
System.Decimal	CURRENCY
1-dimensional arrays	SAFEARRAY
Value types	Equivalently named struct

Table D-1. C# type to COM type mapping (continued)

C# type	COM type
enum	Equivalently named enum
interface	Equivalently named interface
class	Equivalently named CoClass

a COM dates are less precise, causing comparison problems.

Table D-2 shows the mapping of the C# modifiers to their equivalent COM interface attributes.

Table D-2. C# modifier/COM attribute mapping

C# modifier	COM attribute
<no modifier>	[in]
out	[out]
ref	[in, out]
<return value>	[out, retval]

Working with Assemblies

This appendix describes a number of useful techniques for working with assemblies. Among the topics covered are how to create modules, how to manage the global assembly cache, how to make assemblies shareable, and how to use the *nmake* utility to automate your builds.

Building Shareable Assemblies

For most applications you build components that are either standalone assembly EXEs or DLLs. If you want to build shareable components that are shared across multiple applications, you need to give your assembly a strong name (using the *sn* utility) and install it into the global cache (using the *gacutil* utility).

Building Modules

The *al* utility doesn't rebuild assemblies from other assemblies, so you need to compile your C# files as modules, using the flag (*/target:module*). Here's an example:

```
csc /target:module a.cs
```

Linking Modules to Assemblies

Once your modules are built, you can create a single shared assembly with the *al* (*alink*) utility. You specify the name of the new assembly and the source modules. Here's an example:

```
al /out:c.dll a.netmodule b.netmodule
```

Building with Your New Assemblies

You can now create applications with the new assembly by referencing it on the compiler command line. For example:

```
csc /r:c.dll d.cs
```

Note that in order to use classes within the namespaces contained in the *c.dll* assembly of the preceding example, you need to specify the using keyword to reference the namespace.

Sharing Assemblies

To share assemblies across multiple applications where the assembly itself doesn't reside in the same directory, you need to install it into the assembly cache. To install an assembly into the cache, it must be signed with a strong name. The sequence is:

1. You must generate a key file. For example:

   ```
   sn -k key.snk
   ```

2. Then build an assembly that is signed with the strong name:

   ```
   al /out:e.dll /keyfile:key.snk a.netmodule b.netmodule
   ```

3. Once your assembly is signed, you can install it in the global assembly cache.

Note that installing an assembly to the shared cache doesn't copy it to anywhere, so when specifying the reference on compilations, you need to specify the assembly file location for the compiler:

```
csc /r:..\e.dll f.cs
```

Managing the Global Assembly Cache

There are two ways to work with the assembly cache. One is with the Windows Explorer, which has a shell extension that displays the cache and allows you to manipulate the entries. If you explore the *%SYSTEMROOT%\ assembly* directory, you can display the current cache:

```
start %SYSTEMROOT%\assembly
```

Alternatively you can use the *gacutil* utility, which allows you to install, uninstall, and list the contents of the global assembly cache. The following:

```
gacutil /i e.dll
```

installs *e.dll*.

This example:

```
gacutil /u e
```

uninstalls all assemblies with the name e.

This example:

```
gacutil /u e,ver=0.0.0.0
```

uninstalls only the assembly e that matches the version number.

Using nmake

You can use *nmake* to automate many tasks that build assemblies and modules. Here's an example that shows many of the previous command lines in a cohesive manner. Particular *nmake* features to note are the use of the .SUFFIXES keyword to add a definition for the *.cs* file extension and the use of the response file with the C# compiler, for when more source file names are supplied than can be listed on the command line.

```
REF=/r:c.dll
DEBUG=/debug
.SUFFIXES: .exe .dll .cs .netmodule
.cs.netmodule:
        csc /t:module $*.cs
.cs.exe:
        csc $(DEBUG) $(REF) @<<big.tmp
$*.cs $(SRCLIST)
<<
all : d.exe f.exe
d.exe : d.cs c.dll
c.dll : a.netmodule b.netmodule
    al /out:c.dll a.netmodule b.netmodule
b.netmodule : b.cs
a.netmodule : a.cs
key.snk :
        sn -k $*.snk
e.dll : a.netmodule b.netmodule key.snk
    al /out:$*.dll /keyfile:key.snk a.netmodule b.netmodule
    gacutil /i $*.dll
f.exe : f.cs e.dll
    csc $(DEBUG) /r:.\e.dll f.cs
clean:
    gacutil /u e
    del key.snk *.netmodule c.dll d.exe e.dll f.exe *.pdb /q
```

APPENDIX F
Namespaces and Assemblies

This appendix allows you to look up a namespace and determine which assemblies export that namespace. This information is helpful when constructing the appropriate /reference:<*file list*> command-line option for the C# compiler. Note that *mscorlib.dll* is implicitly referenced by the compiler unless the /nostdlib command-line option is used.

Namespace	DLLs
Accessibility	*Accessibility.dll*
EnvDTE	*envdte.dll*
IEHost.Execute	*IEExecRemote.dll*
Microsoft.CLRAdmin	*mscorcfg.dll*
Microsoft.CSharp	*cscompmgd.dll*
	System.dll
Microsoft.IE	*IEHost.dll*
	IIEHost.dll
Microsoft.JScript	*Microsoft.JScript.dll*
Microsoft.JScript.Vsa	*Microsoft.JScript.dll*
Microsoft.Office.Core	*office.dll*
Microsoft.VisualBasic	*Microsoft.VisualBasic.dll*
	System.dll
Microsoft.VisualBasic.Compatibility.VB6	*Microsoft.VisualBasic.Compatibility.Data.dll*
	Microsoft.VisualBasic.Compatibility.dll
Microsoft.VisualBasic.CompilerServices	*Microsoft.VisualBasic.dll*
Microsoft.VisualBasic.Vsa	*Microsoft.VisualBasic.Vsa.dll*
Microsoft.VisualC	*Microsoft.VisualC.Dll*

Namespace	DLLs
Microsoft.Vsa	*Microsoft.JScript.dll*
	Microsoft.Vsa.dll
Microsoft.Vsa.Vb.CodeDOM	*Microsoft.Vsa.Vb.CodeDOMProcessor.dll*
Microsoft.Win32	*mscorlib.dll*
	System.dll
Microsoft_VsaVb	*Microsoft_VsaVb.dll*
RegCode	*RegCode.dll*
System	*mscorlib.dll*
	System.dll
System.CodeDom	*System.dll*
System.CodeDom.Compiler	*System.dll*
System.Collections	*mscorlib.dll*
System.Collections.Specialized	*System.dll*
System.ComponentModel	*System.dll*
System.ComponentModel.Design	*System.Design.dll*
	System.dll
System.ComponentModel.Design.Serialization	*System.Design.dll*
	System.dll
System.Configuration	*System.dll*
System.Configuration.Assemblies	*mscorlib.dll*
System.Configuration.Install	*System.Configuration.Install.dll*
System.Data	*System.Data.dll*
System.Data.Common	*System.Data.dll*
System.Data.OleDb	*System.Data.dll*
System.Data.SqlClient	*System.Data.dll*
System.Data.SqlTypes	*System.Data.dll*
System.Diagnostics	*mscorlib.dll*
	System.Configuration.Install.dll
System.Diagnostics.Design	*System.Design.dll*
System.Diagnostics.SymbolStore	*ISymWrapper.dll*
	mscorlib.dll
System.DirectoryServices	*System.DirectoryServices.dll*
System.Drawing	*System.Drawing.dll*
System.Drawing.Design	*System.Drawing.Design.dll*
	System.Drawing.dll

Namespace	DLLs
System.Drawing.Drawing2D	*System.Drawing.dll*
System.Drawing.Imaging	*System.Drawing.dll*
System.Drawing.Printing	*System.Drawing.dll*
System.Drawing.Text	*System.Drawing.dll*
System.EnterpriseServices	*System.EnterpriseServices.dll*
System.EnterpriseServices. CompensatingResourceManager	*System.EnterpriseServices.dll*
System.EnterpriseServices.Internal	*System.EnterpriseServices.dll*
System.Globalization	*mscorlib.dll*
System.IO	*mscorlib.dll* *System.dll*
System.IO.IsolatedStorage	*mscorlib.dll*
System.Management	*System.Management.dll*
System.Management. Instrumentation	*System.Management.dll*
System.Messaging	*System.Messaging.dll*
System.Messaging.Design	*System.Design.dll* *System.Messaging.dll*
System.Net	*System.dll*
System.Net.Sockets	*System.dll*
System.Reflection	*mscorlib.dll*
System.Reflection.Emit	*mscorlib.dll*
System.Resources	*mscorlib.dll* *System.Windows.Forms.dll*
System.Runtime.CompilerServices	*mscorlib.dll*
System.Runtime. InteropServices	*mscorlib.dll*
System.Runtime.InteropServices. CustomMarshalers	*CustomMarshalers.dll*
System.Runtime.InteropServices. Expando	*mscorlib.dll*
System.Runtime.Remoting	*mscorlib.dll*
System.Runtime.Remoting.Activation	*mscorlib.dll*
System.Runtime.Remoting.Channels	*mscorlib.dll* *System.Runtime.Remoting.dll*
System.Runtime.Remoting.Channels.Http	*System.Runtime.Remoting.dll*
System.Runtime.Remoting.Channels.Tcp	*System.Runtime.Remoting.dll*
System.Runtime.Remoting.Contexts	*mscorlib.dll*

Namespace	DLLs
System.Runtime.Remoting.Lifetime	*mscorlib.dll*
System.Runtime.Remoting.Messaging	*mscorlib.dll*
System.Runtime.Remoting.Metadata	*mscorlib.dll*
System.Runtime.Remoting.Metadata.W3cXsd2001	*mscorlib.dll*
System.Runtime.Remoting.MetadataServices	*System.Runtime.Remoting.dll*
System.Runtime.Remoting.Proxies	*mscorlib.dll*
System.Runtime.Remoting.Services	*mscorlib.dll* *System.Runtime.Remoting.dll*
System.Runtime.Serialization	*mscorlib.dll*
System.Runtime.Serialization.Formatters	*mscorlib.dll*
System.Runtime.Serialization.Formatters.Binary	*mscorlib.dll*
System.Runtime.Serialization.Formatters.Soap	*System.Runtime.Serialization.Formatters.Soap.dll*
System.Security	*mscorlib.dll*
System.Security.Cryptography	*mscorlib.dll*
System.Security.Cryptography.X509Certificates	*mscorlib.dll* *System.dll*
System.Security.Cryptography.Xml	*System.Security.dll*
System.Security.Permissions	*mscorlib.dll* *System.dll*
System.Security.Policy	*mscorlib.dll*
System.Security.Principal	*mscorlib.dll*
System.ServiceProcess	*System.ServiceProcess.dll*
System.ServiceProcess.Design	*System.Design.dll* *System.ServiceProcess.dll*
System.Text	*mscorlib.dll*
System.Text.RegularExpressions	*System.dll*
System.Threading	*mscorlib.dll* *System.dll*
System.Timers	*System.dll*
System.Web	*System.Web.dll*
System.Web.Caching	*System.Web.dll*
System.Web.Configuration	*System.Web.dll*

Namespace	DLLs
System.Web.Handlers	System.Web.dll
System.Web.Hosting	System.Web.dll
System.Web.Mail	System.Web.dll
System.Web.RegularExpressions	System.Web.RegularExpressions.dll
System.Web.Security	System.Web.dll
System.Web.Services	System.Web.Services.dll
System.Web.Services.Configuration	System.Web.Services.dll
System.Web.Services.Description	System.Web.Services.dll
System.Web.Services.Discovery	System.Web.Services.dll
System.Web.Services.Protocols	System.Web.Services.dll
System.Web.SessionState	System.Web.dll
System.Web.UI	System.Web.dll
System.Web.UI.Design	System.Design.dll
System.Web.UI.Design.WebControls	System.Design.dll
System.Web.UI.HtmlControls	System.Web.dll
System.Web.UI.WebControls	System.Web.dll
System.Web.Util	System.Web.dll
System.Windows.Forms	System.Windows.Forms.dll
System.Windows.Forms.ComponentModel.Com2Interop	System.Windows.Forms.dll
System.Windows.Forms.Design	System.Design.dll System.Windows.Forms.dll
System.Windows.Forms.PropertyGridInternal	System.Windows.Forms.dll
System.Xml	System.Data.dll System.XML.dll
System.Xml.Schema	System.XML.dll
System.Xml.Serialization	System.XML.dll
System.Xml.XPath	System.XML.dll
System.Xml.Xsl	System.XML.dll

Index

Symbols

@ (identifier prefix)
  identifiers, 6
  verbatim string literals and, 13
+ (addition) operator, 46
  precedence of, 19
  relevance to enums, 61
= (assignment) operator
  precedence of, 20
  relevance to enums, 61
! XML type ID prefix, 82
& (bitwise and) operator, 46
  address-of, returning a pointer, 74
  enums, relevance to, 61
  precedence of, 19
^ (bitwise for) operator, 46
  precedence of, 20
  relevance to enums, 61
\' char type, 12
\\ char type, 12
\\" char type, 12
?: (conditional ternary)
  precedence of, 20
  using three-state logic operators, 48
-- (decrement) operator, 46
  precedence of, 19
  relevance to enums, 61
/ (division) operator, 46
/ (division) operator, precedence of, 20
% (division remainder) operator, 46
  precedence of, 20
/// (documentation comments), 78

. (dot)
  x.y (member access), 19
== (equals) operator, 46
  Equals () method and, 85
  precedence of, 20
  preprocess directives and, 77
  relevance to enums, 61
> (greater than) operator, 46
  precedence of, 20
  relevance to enums, 61
++ (increment) operator, 46
  precedence of, 19
  relevance to enums, 61
+? lazy quanifiers, in regular
      expressions, 101
*? lazy quantifiers, in regular
      expressions, 101
?? lazy quantifiers, in regular
      expressions, 101
< (less than) operator, 46
  precedence of, 20
  relevance to enums, 61
* (multiplication) operator, 46
  dereference, 74
  precedence of, 19
! (not) operator, 46
  precedence of, 19
!= operator, 46
  Equals () method and, 85
  precedence of, 20
  preprocessor directives and, 77
  relevance to enums, 61
&& operator, 49

We'd like to hear your suggestions for improving our indexes. Send email to *index@oreilly.com.*

GACUtil.exe (global assembly cache utility), 159
garbage collectors (GCs), 133
  cleanup of non-memory resources, 53
GCs (see garbage collectors)
generations, in garbage collecting, 134
generic request/response architecture, 107
get keyword, 165
GetCustomAttribute method, retrieving a custom attribute at runtime, 132
GetHashCode() method, 85
GetLength method, returning number of elements, 59
GetType() method, 86
global assembly cache
  GACUtil.exe utility, 159
  managing, 182
global namespace, 31
globalization, 154
goto label statement, using switch statements, 24
goto statements, 27, 165
  using switch statements, 24
graphics, 152
Group class, 102
GUI debugger (DbgClr.exe), 159
Guid attribute, 146

H

Hashtable class, 96, 148
Hejlsberg, Anders (co-creator of C# language), 1
HTTP-specific support, 108

I

I1/I2/I4/I8 enum values for UnmanagedType, 142
ICloneable interface, 88
  core types and, 148
ICollection interface, 99
IComparable interface, 89
  core types and, 148
IComparer interface, 99
IConvertible interface
  core types and, 148
identifiers, 6

IDictionary interface, 100
IDictionaryEnumerator interface, 100
IDispatch enum value for UnmanagedType, 142
IEnumerable interface, 97
  foreach loops and, 26
IEnumerator interface, 98
if statement, 165
#if symbol preprocessor directive, 77
if-else statements, 23
IFormattable interface, 90
  core types and, 148
IHashCodeProvider interface, 101
ILAsm.exe
  disassembler, for exploring BLC, 147
  MSIL assembler, 159
ILDasm.exe (MSIL disassembler), 159
IList interface, 95, 100
implicit conversions, 7, 48
implicit operator, 165
imutable strings, 92
In attribute, 142
in operator, 165
<include> XML tag, 81
inclusive (minimum) value, 91
indexing strings, 94
inheritance, 31–36
InnerException argument, 71
input/output, 103–107
  directories and files, 106
  FCL and, 148
InstallUtil.exe (installer utility), 159
instances, 121
  constructors, 49
  members, 7, 39
int integral type, 9, 165, 179
integral conversions, 9
integral types, 9
Interface enum value for UnmanagedType, 142
interfaces, 55–58, 95
  collections, 97–101
  conversions, 58
  defining, 55
  delegates, comparing with, 63
  explicitly implementing, 57
  extending, 56
  ICloneable/IComparable, 89
  IFormattable, 90
  implementing, 55

P

\<param\> XML tag
  user-defining, 81
P XML type ID prefix, 82
pack size, 139
packaging of assemblies, 116
packing-size parameter for StructLayout
      attribute, 141
\<para\> XML tag, 81
\<param\> XML tag, 80
ParamIndex, for formatting strings, 93
\<paramref\> XML tag, 81
params parameter modifiers, 166
  in delegate declaration, 62
pause time, in garbage collecting, 134
PE (Portable Executable) files,
      packaging, 116
\<permission\> XML tag, 80
PEVerify.exe (portable executable
      verifier), 159
picture format specifiers, 175
PInvoke (Platform Invocation
      Services), 137
placeholders, 22
Platform Invocation Services
      (PInvoke), 137
Point class, using types, 30
pointer types, 8, 73–77
pointer-to-member (->) operator, 74
polymorphism, 32
Portable Executable (PE) files,
      packaging, 116
portable executable verifier
      (PEVerify.exe), 159
Position property, 104
positional parameter, 72
precedence, of operators, 18
predefined types, 8–13
    bool, 12
    char, 11
    decimal, 11
    floating-point, 10
    integral, 9
    object, 12
    string, 13
predinined attributes, 128
preprocessor directives, 77
PreserveSig parameter, for DllImport
      attribute, 140

primary operators, precedence of, 19
primitive types, 18
private access modifiers, 36, 166
private assemblies, 117
ProgId attribute, 146
programming, 84–146
    assemblies for, 115–119
    collections for, 95–101
    common types for, 84
    custom attributes for, 126–132
    input/output for, 103–107
    Interop with Native DLLs
          for, 137–143
    math, supporting language
          for, 90–91
    networking for, 107–111
    reflection for, 119–126
    regular expressions for, 101
    strings for, 92–94
    threads for, 111–115
programming models, 107
property field, 41
protected access modifier, 36, 166
protected internal access modifier, 36
protocol handlers
    adding new, 109
    configuring requests, 108
pseudo-custom attributes, compiling
      custom attributes, 127
public access modifier, 36, 166
Pulse methods, 115
pulse operations, 113
PulseAll methods, 115

Q

Queue class, 96, 148

R

\<return value\> modifier, 180
\<revision\> assembly version
      numbers, 117
\r char type, 12
R4 enum value for
      UnmanagedType, 142
R8 enum value for
      UnmanagedType, 142
Random class, 91
RCW (Runtime Callable Wrapper), 143
readonly field modifiers, 41, 166

U

U1/U2/U4/U8 enum values for
  UnmanagedType, 142
UDP (User Datagram Protocol), 107
  using, 109
uint integral type, 9, 168, 179
ulong integral type, 9, 168, 179
unary operators, precedence of, 19
unboxing value types, 16
unchecked (arithmetic check off)
  operator, 19, 168
#undef symbol preprocessor
  directive, 77
underscore (_) (identifiers), 6
undocumented types, 156
Unicode characters
  representing char types, 11
  representing string types, 13
unified type system, 2, 15–17
Uniform Resource Indicator (see URI)
Unix snarf utility, 108
unmanaged code, 76
  callbacks from, 139
  FCL (Framework Class Library)
    and, 155
UnmanagedType enum values, 142
unsafe code, 73–77
unsafe modifier, 168
unsigned integers, 9
upcasting classes, 32
URI (Uniform Resource Indicator), 107
User Datagram Protocol (see UDP)
user-defined tags, 81
ushort integral type, 9, 168, 179
using keyword, 30, 168
using statement, 28

V

\v char type, 12
value keyword, 168
value types, 8
  boxing and unboxing, 16
  memory for, 13
  simple types and, 15
<value> XML tag, 81
ValueType type, 147, 179
variables, 17
  assigning, 17
  default values for, 18

VariantBool enum value for
  UnmanagedType, 142
VBByRefStr enum value for
  UnmanagedType, 142
verbatim string literals, 13
version numbers (assembly), 117
versioning
  as a C# language feature, 2
  as a CLR feature, 3
  with constants, 41
  virtual function members, 35
virtual function members, 33
  versioning, 35
virtual keyword, 168
void keyword, 168
void* keyword, 76
volatile keyword, 40, 168

W

wait methods, 115
wait operations, 113
#warning text preprocessor
  directive, 78
web-based applications, 153
WebRequestFactory, creating protocol
  for requests, 107
while loop statement, 25, 48, 168
Wiltamuth, Scott (cocreator of C#
  language), 1
WinCV.exe, 160
  for exploring BCLs, 147
windows class viewer (WinCV.exe), as a
  .NET tool, 160
Wsdl.exe (web services description
  language tool), 160

X

XML documentation, 78–82
  FCL (Framework Class Library)
    and, 152
  files, 79
  predefined tags, 80–82
  type/member cross references, 82
  user-defined tags, 81
XML schema definition tool
  (Xsd.exe), 161
Xsd.exe (XML schema definition
  tool), 161

About the Author

Ben Albahari is cofounder of Genamics, a provider of tools for C# and J++ programmers, as well as software for DNA and protein sequence analysis. He is the author of "A Comparative Overview of C#", a frequently cited comparison of C# with C/C++ and Java (*http://www.genamics.com/ visualj++/csharp_comparative.htm*) that was recently named one of the top 10 .NET sites by DevX (*http://www.devx.com/dotnet/resources/vsresources-17.asp*). Ben is a resident of Perth, Australia, and in his spare time enjoys composing music on his computer. He can be reached at *ben@genamics.com*.

Peter Drayton is an independent consultant, helping early-stage companies define and build systems that take advantage of technologies such as .NET, SOAP, XML, and COM+. Peter is also an instructor and course author for DevelopMentor, teaching C# and .NET classes. Originally from Cape Town, South Africa, Peter now lives in the San Francisco Bay area with his wife, Julie. He spends his spare time researching .NET and tinkering with a small flotilla of computers cluttering up their apartment. He can be reached at *peter@razorsoft.com*.

Brad Merrill works as a software engineer in the .NET Framework Integration team at Microsoft. He previously worked as a software engineer at Digital Equipment Corporation and Sybase. His areas of expertise are in distributed systems, transaction processing, operating systems, and compiler technology. Brad lives in Redmond, Washington, and is an avid tournament chess player and bridge player. He can be reached at *zbrad@gte.net* or *http://www.cybercom.net/~zbrad*.

Colophon

Our look is the result of reader comments, our own experimentation, and feedback from distribution channels. Distinctive covers complement our distinctive approach to technical topics, breathing personality and life into potentially dry subjects.

The animals on the cover of *C# Essentials* are star-nosed moles (*Condylura cristata*). Like all moles, star-nosed moles live primarily in underground tunnels that they dig, but they do surface to find food. A mole's rodent-like body is covered in short, waterproof gray fur, and it is about six to eight inches long. A notable feature is its long claws, which are perfect for digging its trenches and foraging for food. It has small ears and eyes, and sharp, pointed teeth. A mole's eyesight and hearing are known to be terrible.

The star-nosed mole gets its name from the approximately 25 feelers on its nose that help it find food, primarily insects, worms, and small fish, as well as other small pond life. The star-nosed mole is the best swimmer in the mole family and can even dive to catch a fish. It prefers to live in wetlands but can be found in various areas of the northeastern United States and southeastern Canada.

Moles are mammals who nurse their young, and a female mole has one litter of three to six babies per year.

This particular type of mole is considered to be less of a household pest than its mole cousins because its mostly aquatic diet keeps it from rummaging around in backyards for food.

Darren Kelly was the production editor, and Mary Anne Weeks Mayo was the copyeditor for *C# Essentials*. Matt Hutchinson and Claire Cloutier provided quality control. Joe Wizda wrote the index.

Ellie Volckhausen designed the cover of this book, based on a series design by Edie Freedman. The cover image is an original engraving from *The Illustrated Natural History* by J. G. Wood, published in 1865. Emma Colby and Melanie Wang produced the cover layout with QuarkXPress 4.1 using Adobe's ITC Garamond font.

David Futato designed the interior layout. Neil Walls converted the files from Microsoft Word to FrameMaker 5.5.6, using tools created by Mike Sierra. The text font is Linotype Birka; the heading font is Adobe Myriad Condensed; and the code font is LucasFont's TheSans Mono Condensed. The illustrations that appear in the book were produced by Robert Romano and Jessamyn Read using Macromedia FreeHand 9 and Adobe Photoshop 6. The tip and warning icons were drawn by Christopher Bing. This colophon was written by Nicole Arigo.